河南省高等学校青年骨干教师资助计划项目

英汉隐喻句对比研究

姜　玲著

A Contrastive Study of Metaphorical Sentences in English and Chinese

河南大学出版社

图书在版编目（CIP）数据

英汉隐喻句对比研究 / 姜玲著. —开封：河南大学出版社，2008.5

（英语博士文库）

ISBN 978-7-81091-818-3

Ⅰ. 英… Ⅱ. 姜… Ⅲ. 隐喻—句法—对比研究—英语、汉语 Ⅳ. H146.3　H314.3

中国版本图书馆 CIP 数据核字（2008）第 066861 号

责任编辑　薛巧玲

封面设计　马　龙

出　　版　河南大学出版社

地址：河南省开封市明伦街 85 号　　邮编：475001

电话：0378-2825001（营销部）　　网址：www.hupress.com

排　　版　理光文印设计中心

印　　刷　河南省瑞光印务股份有限公司

版　　次　2008 年 5 月第 1 版　　**印　　次**　2008 年 5 月第 1 次印刷

开　　本　650mm×960mm　1/16　　**印　　张**　12.50

字　　数　168 千字　　**印　　数**　1—2000 册

定　　价　23.00 元

（本书如有印装质量问题请与河南大学出版社营销部联系调换）

序　言

从事语言学研究以来，我先后出版了几部著作，其中包括《英汉比较语法纲要》、《英语句型的动态研究》、《思想模块假说》、《英汉语信息结构对比研究》等。但每部书出版之后，我都会有新的发现，想把它重新写过，却没有足够的时间和精力。1997年，我在指导杨莉藜的博士论文时，又一次萌发了修改《英语句型的动态研究》一书的念头。因为杨莉藜的论文使我认识到，句子的生成机制除了捏合机制、代换机制和转换机制外，还应该包括隐喻机制。2000年，我招收了最后一名博士研究生，就是现在的姜玲博士。巧合的是，她对隐喻也很感兴趣。不仅如此，她还对英语语法的研究很感兴趣，曾经仔细钻研过夸克等四位学者编著的《当代英语语法》和《英语语法大全》，发表过数篇与英语语法有关的论文，而且正在编写专著。一年之后，她进行博士论文选题时，有两个课题。一个是“英汉隐喻句对比研究”，一个是“英汉存在句对比研究”。这两个选题都很好，都很有新意。相比之下，第二个要容易写一些，因为她在广泛查阅了前人研究成果之后发现，没有人系统地运用功能语言学的三大元功能对英汉存在句进行过对比研究。这样，整个论文的可操作性很强，结构布局也比较容易把握。而我主张她选择第一个，尽管它要难得多。难处有三。第一，隐喻句好像从来没有人研究过，甚至没有人把它作为一个专门术语使用过。其次，隐喻句既涉及修辞，也涉及语法，要求作者必须有比较广博的知识面。第三，从对比的角度分析，要求作者必须有比较扎实的英汉语功底。让我感到十分欣慰的是，姜玲不仅没有退却，而且知难而进，果断地接受了我的建议，勇敢地选择了第一个课题。

2003 年春节前夕，我读完了姜玲的论文初稿后，十分感动。一年多的时间，要做完一篇博士论文实在不容易，要做出一篇高质量的博士论文更不容易，而姜玲做到了。她在完成学院布置的一些额外工作之后，在兼顾好家庭孩子之后做到了。

从论文中可以看出，姜玲阅读了大量的中外书籍，对国内外有关隐喻和句法研究的主要文献都有较好的理解和运用。人们常常认为，一篇论文中最好只使用一种理论，忌讳使用两种或多种理论，而姜玲却能把三种理论（原型模型论、语法隐喻理论和认知隐喻理论）有机地结合起来，表明她有很强的驾驭能力和科研能力。

博士论文贵在创新，姜玲的博士论文有以下创新。第一，在前人研究的基础上，探讨隐喻在句子形成中的作用，进而提出隐喻是句子形成的一种机制，从而把隐喻和句法结合起来，拓展了句法和隐喻的研究。第二，从客观现实中的各种实体及其相互关系和活动形式出发，探讨及物性系统，并将它改造成 8 个过程，创造性地发展了韩礼德系统功能语言学的重要组成部分——及物性系统。第三，系统、深入地比较了英汉隐喻句的生成机制和表现形式，并将研究成果及时运用到翻译实践中。第一点创新同时也证实了我的设想，使我们有机会合作重新修订《英语句型的动态研究》一书（清华大学出版社 2005 年出版）。

由于上述原因，当姜玲告诉我，她的博士论文要修改成书出版并请我作序时，我欣然答应了。我相信，她对该课题的研究肯定会对国内该领域的研究具有一定的推动作用，对英汉语言教学和英汉互译有一定的指导意义。同时，我也希望，姜玲以此研究为起点，继续关注本课题的研究，做出更大更有意义的成绩。

张　今

2008年1月

前　言

本书主要以原型模型理论及认知语言学理论为指导，对英汉隐喻句进行对比研究，试图对英汉隐喻句的生成机制及体现形式加以探讨，从而说明英汉隐喻句在生成机制及体现形式方面的异同。本研究旨在阐明隐喻像捏合机制、代换机制和转化机制一样，也是一种句子生成机制。

隐喻是语言中的普遍现象，自古就受到研究界的重视。特别是20世纪30年代以来，对隐喻的研究更呈多元化趋势。人们从哲学、逻辑学、社会学、符号学、现象学、阐释学、心理学、语用学等多个学科、多个角度对隐喻的本质、工作机制及作用进行研究。80年代兴起的认知语言学则把隐喻看作一种思维现象，认为它存在于我们生活的各个方面。但是把隐喻和句法结合起来进行研究的还为数不多。虽然以韩礼德为代表的系统功能语法学派提出了“语法隐喻”这一新颖的术语，他们的目的是为了说明，对隐喻的解码会影响词汇语法的选择，所以隐喻既是一种词汇现象，也是一种语法现象，或者说是一种词汇语法现象。本书在前人研究的基础上，探讨隐喻在句子形成中的作用，进而提出隐喻是一种句子生成机制，通过隐喻生成的句子是隐喻句，直接反映客观现实及心理现实的句子是非隐喻句。本书对隐喻和句法的研究是一种补充，具有一定的理论意义和现实意义。

全书共分六个部分。

第一章论述了研究的主题、理论框架、主要目的，并对隐喻句进行了界定。

张今先生认为，虽然语言中的句子千变万化，但语言中都存在着一些基本句型，这些基本句型都是与客观世界和心理世界相对应的，它们直接反映和描写客观现实，其他的句子都是派生句，是基本句型通过捏合、代换和转化生成的。这一精辟论述科学而系统地解释了语言中绝大多数句子之间的关系，但对有些句子之间关系的解释力还不够充分。于是，作者在前人研究的基础上，大胆地提出了隐喻也是一种句子生成机制的设想。作者明确地把隐喻句定义为谓语动词与主语和/或宾语/补语之间的关系与客观现实中动作与主体和/或客体/属性之间的关系不一致的句子。也就是说，隐喻句中所表示的句子成分之间的关系和客观现实中实体之间的关系不一致。这种不一致可以表现在下列关系中：主语和动词的关系，动词和宾语的关系，主语、动词和宾语之间的关系，主语、动词和补语之间的关系。

第二章运用对比的方法系统地论述了英汉隐喻句的生成机制。

认知语言学认为，隐喻是一种思维现象，隐喻就是在思想上把一事物体验为另一事物，这是概念隐喻。概念隐喻反映在语言中就是隐喻表达，表现在句法上就是隐喻句。由于人类共同的认知模式和思维定势，英汉隐喻句的生成机制基本相同，都表现为把抽象的事物隐喻为具体的事物。具体的事物可以分为人、动物、植物和物体，故英汉隐喻句的生成机制可分别表现为拟人、拟动物、拟植物、拟物和异化。但是，英语和汉语毕竟分属两个截然不同的语系，是两个完全不同的民族所使用的语言，也就必然带有各自的社会、文化以及心理等方面的特点，英汉隐喻句的生成机制也会表现出各自的特点。

第三章和第四章从对比的角度探讨了英汉隐喻句的体现形式。

人们对客观世界的认识不只停留在一个个具体事物上，同时还涉及事物的属性、特征以及一事物与他事物的关系等等，这一切在语言中都表现为及物性系统。及物性系统是韩礼德系统功能语言学的重要组成部分，是语言表述功能或概念功能的具体体现。但本书中的及物性系统虽然是受韩礼德的启发提出的，却和韩礼德的及物性系统有很大的不同。韩礼德主要从过程本身对语言的及物性系统进行描述，阐明语言具有六大过程系统，即物质过程、心理过程、关系过程、行为过程、言语过程和存在过程，其中，物质过程、心理过程和关系过程是主要过程，行为过程、言语过程和存在过程是次要过程。本书则从客观现实中的各种实体及其相互关系和活动形式出发探讨及物性系统，把及物性系统划分为八个过程，即物质过程、抽象实体过程、感官过程、行为过程、思维过程、言语过程、关系过程和存在过程。物质过程表示非生命物质实体的物理活动；抽象实体过程表示抽象实体的抽象活动；感官过程表示有生命体的感官活动和感情活动；行为过程表示有生命体，特别是人的动作行为；思维过程和言语过程只能表示人的思维行为和言语行为；关系过程表示物质实体之间的关系；存在过程表示物质实体的客观存在。

对各个过程的论述清楚地阐明了每个过程所表示的意义。每个过程都用来表达特定的语义，包含特定的语义成分，涉及特定的参与者。它们是每个过程的常规形式。但在语言的实际运用过程中，每个过程并不总是表示特定的语义，它们常常被用来表示其他过程所表示的语义，使过程中的参与者与动作之间的关系不一致，从而形成隐喻句。动作与参与者之间的不一致关系，既可以表现在主谓关系上，也可以表现在动宾关系上，还可以表现在主动宾/补关系上。

人类具有基本相同的认知模式和心理感受，所以，英汉隐喻句的体现形式基本相同，都表现为把比较抽象的过程隐喻为比较具体的过程，也就是说，用比较具体的物质实体的过程表示比较抽象的抽象实体的过程。所以，所有关于物质实体，包括有生命体和无生命体的过程，几乎都可以被投射到抽象实体过程，而抽象实体过程却不能向物质实体过程投射。当然，由于英汉两种语言本身的差异及其不同使用者在文化心理方面的差异，英汉隐喻句的体现形式不可能完全相同，特别是在主谓及物过程和主谓宾/补及物过程中表现出很大的差异。这是因为汉语中的有灵动词和无灵动词界限分明，而英语中的有灵动词和无灵动词界限模糊。在汉民族文化中，人及由人组成的社会组织是一切行为的发出者，只有人或人类社会组织才具有行为能力，所以汉语中很多动词都要求人或人类社会组织作主语，这些动词被称为有灵动词。而在英语中，有灵动词和无灵动词界限很不分明，许多动词既可以要求人或人类社会组织作主语，也可以允许无生命实体或抽象实体甚至非实体如动作、行为、事件、事实等作主语。

第五章论述了英语隐喻句的汉译问题。正如在第三章和第四章中所述，汉语中的有灵动词和无灵动词界限分明，许多在英语中表现为主谓之间或主谓宾/补之间的隐喻句翻译成汉语时，只能译成非隐喻句。它们可以分别译成汉语的有灵主语句、复合句、并列句、无主句、不定人称句和无灵主语句。至于动宾及物性系统不一致的隐喻句，汉译时常常使用原有的主语，对谓语部分进行适当的调整，有时也可以改变句子的主语，以适应汉语表达习惯。

第六章对全书进行了总结，既作出了一些尝试性的结论，同时也指出了可能存在的问题以及今后的努力方向。

总之，本书通过对英汉隐喻句的对比研究，证实了作者的设想，说明隐喻确实是句子生成机制之一。英汉语中都存在着大量因隐喻而产生的隐喻句。同时，本书也发现英汉隐喻句在生成机制及体现形式上既具有一定的共性，也具有一定的差异。但由于笔者的水平有限，本书的缺点与错误在所难免，恳请各位前辈、同仁不吝赐教，批评指正。

姜　玲

2008 年 1 月

Contents

Chapter One

Introduction

1.1 Introductory Remarks

In the first book in China on theoretical contrastive linguistics between English and Chinese (王菊泉，1982：2), Zhang Jin (张今、陈云清，1981) makes a thorough study of syntactic structures in the two languages. He attempts to study the generative mechanisms of sentence patterns in the two languages.

Armed with Marxism, Zhang Jin sticks to the principle of the dialectical relationship of reality, language and thinking. He insists that reality is the base of thinking while thinking actively reflects reality through language. Therefore, he concludes that syntactic structure is determined by three factors: a) reality; b) perspective and order that the mind takes to reflect the reality; and c) the degree to which the mind conceptualizes the reality and the different methods used to symbolize the conceptualization (张今、陈云清，1981: 7). Hence, if the mind conceptualizes the reality directly and factually, language and reality are correspondent. Things or entities are expressed by nouns, attributes by adjectives, actions or motions by verbs, manners and circumstances by adverbs and prepositional phrases. As far as syntax is concerned, all the basic sentence patterns are modeled on the external world directly. The relationship of the elements in the sentences is the reflection of the general relation of the entities in the outside world.

Although the mind reflects reality actively, it may do so from different perspectives and in different order. It may take the substance and its motion as a whole. It may separate the substance and its motion. It may regard the substance and its attributes as a whole or separate them. It may reflect the motion and its token separately or inseparately. All of the different perspectives and orders the mind takes to reflect reality lead to changes of the basic sentence patterns. These changed sentences are considered as derived sentences in language.

According to the above theory, Zhang Jin claims that there are four basic sentence patterns in language: SVP [= SVC], SV, SVO and SVIO [= SVOO] (张今、陈云清，1981: 19, 24). These patterns are in accordance with the basic events in the physical world. They are the direct reflection of the world in the mind. All the other sentences are derived from the basic sentence patterns. They are passive sentences, negative sentences, interrogative sentences, imperative sentences, exclamatory sentences, compound sentences and complex sentences, etc. They are the result of the active reflection of the world in the mind.

Zhang Jin continues his study on the generative mechanisms of sentence patterns. He later claims that there are five basic sentence patterns, adding SVOC to the original four, (张今，1990：2) or six basic sentence patterns, plus there-be construction (张今，1997: 21). Other sentences are generated via combination, substitution and transformation. Transformational mechanism is the core mechanism (张今，1990：2).

Zhang Jin's theory is both scientific and systematic. It is scientific in that it offers a strong historical and logical interpretation to the production of not only the basic sentence patterns but also the derived sentences. It links sentence patterns to reality and offers a dialectical view on the study of sentences. It is systematic in that it connects almost all kinds of sentences and explicates how they are produced, developed and transformed. Consequently, Zhang Jin's theory is of great importance in both theory and practice. Theoretically, his theory explains the relation between grammatical choice and meaning, i.e., reality. One meaning may be expressed in different sentences, such as the active and the passive. His theory also provides criteria for classification. If one wants to know whether a noun after a verb is the Object, he can easily do it by changing the sentence into passive. Practically, Zhang Jin's theory is helpful to the study of syntax. One can start by learning the basic sentence patterns and then learn the derived sentences. Language learners can also be helped to identify the similarities and differences between sentences. Thus they can improve their linguistic competence in expressing, understanding, writing and translating.

Despite all its merits, it seems that Zhang Jin's theory is unable to explain very convincingly the mutual relationship between the following sentences:

(1) Mary saw them at the summit.

(2) The fifth day *saw* them at the summit.

(3) On the fifth day, they arrived at the summit.

(4) They *arrived at* similar conclusions.

At first sight, one can find that these sentences are closely related to one another. (1) and (2), (2) and (3), (3) and (4) all have close relationship. (1) and (2), (3) and (4) are of the same sentence pattern. They are related syntactically. (2) and (3) are of the same (to some extent) meaning, so they are related semantically. If the same meaning (or the same reality) is expressed in different sentence patterns, it must be explained by virtue of the function of the mind. But how does the mind reflect the world so that it can express the meaning with (2) instead of (3)? It seems that none of the three generative mechanisms of Zhang Jin's theory work very well here.

In order to make Zhang Jin's theory more comprehensive and more explicative, the author of this book presumes that she could add to the original three generative devices another one which she makes bold to call "metaphorical mechanism". The author thinks that the four sentences above are really linked to one another. (2) and (4) are modeled on (1) and (3) respectively by virtue of metaphorization, taking *the fifth day* as a person who could see and *conclusions* as a physical entity which occupies a material space. (1) and (3) are the prototypes for (2) and (4). (1) and (3) may be called the prototype sentences. (2) and (4) may be called the model sentences. A model sentence presupposes a prototype sentence. Therefore, the relationship between (1) and (2), (3) and (4) is an embryological one. (2) and (4) generate from (1) and (3). (2) and (3) are connected in meaning since they are synonymous to some extent. (2) is a metaphorical expression while (3) is a literal one. The relationship between (2) and (3) is a synonymous one, namely, a logical one. In our opinion, the embryological relationship is more fundamental than the logical one.

Before a detailed study of metaphorical mechanism, a brief discussion will be made on the literature of metaphorical study to show how the author has been so enlightened as to come to the proposition that metaphorization is one of the generative mechanisms of sentences.

1.2 Literature Review

Metaphor is an important research topic that has drawn scholastic pursuit since remote antiquity. Study on metaphor before the 20th century is usually called the classical period of metaphor study (Yu Ning, 1998: 10; Yan Shiqing, 2000: 13). The classical theories are comparison and substitution. They both view metaphor as a linguistic phenomenon, and assume a fundamental distinction between literal and figurative (or metaphorical) senses. These theories are helpful in understanding metaphorical expressions in language, but they are not inspiring enough for the author to draw the assumption that metaphorization is one of the generative mechanisms of sentences. What has enlightened the author has been the contemporary studies on metaphor. The most important ones are the studies on metaphor in lexicology and lexical semantics, the studies on grammatical metaphor in systemic-functional linguistics and the studies on metaphor in cognitive linguistics.

1.2.1 Studies on Metaphor in Lexicology and Lexical Semantics

Studies on metaphor in lexicology and lexical semantics are mainly concentrated on "the force of metaphor" (Zhang Yunfei, 1987: 285) in semantic extension and formation of lexical items.

According to Zhang Yunfei, "metaphor is a figure of speech containing an implied comparison based on association of similarity, in which a word or a phrase ordinarily and primarily used for one thing is applied to another, a process which often results in semantic change or figurative extension of meaning" (Zhang Yunfei, 1987: 284). Obviously, Zhang Yunfei follows the classical theory, maintaining that metaphor is a figure of speech which is an implied comparison based on association of similarity. This involves the substitution of one word or one phrase for another. However, he continues to argue that metaphor is a process which often results in semantic change or figurative extension of meaning. He regards metaphor as a dynamic process which can lead to semantic extension, as well as a stative linguistic phenomenon. In this sense, metaphor means metaphorization.

Other linguists such as Lu Guoqiang, Wang Rongpei, Li Dong, Lu Xiaojuan, Lyons and Saeed all hold the opinion that metaphor is one of the principal factors operative in semantic change of words (陆国强, 1983: 64; 汪榕培、李冬, 1983: 120, 123; 汪榕培、卢晓娟, 1997: 234; Lyons, 1995: 59-60; Saeed, 1997: 16). Lyons goes on to argue further that "metaphorical creativity ... is part of everyone's linguistic competence" (Lyons, 1995: 60). Thus metaphor is not only a figure of speech, it is a kind of creative ability which can produce new meanings of words. Saeed also finds the generative force of metaphor in the metaphorical extension of words, "where some new idea is depicted in something more familiar" (Saeed, 1997: 16).

The force of metaphor in the formation of lexical items is mainly described in the buildup of compounds. There are two ways of forming compounds by metaphor. One is by using a word in its metaphorical sense. The other is an implied comparison (汪榕培、李冬, 1983: 19; 汪榕培、卢晓娟, 1997: 42). Compounds such as *eardrum, eyeball, armpit, footnote* are formed by describing one thing to mean another. *Drum, ball, pit* and *foot* are all used metaphorically out of their normal literal sense. Compounds like *grass-green, pitch-dark, snow-white* are implied comparison, which is the main characteristic of metaphor. They can be extended to similes, meaning *as green as grass, as dark as pitch, as white as snow*.

While metaphor is a functional force in the formation and semantic broadening of words, can it be a force in the generation of sentences? Our answer is a positive yes, as will be illustrated later in the book.

1.2.2 Studies on Grammatical Metaphor in Systemic-Functional Linguistics

Grammatical metaphor is proposed by Halliday, the founder of systemic-functional linguistics. Halliday thinks that metaphor is "variation in the expression of meaning"(Halliday, 1994: 341, 342). Since "lexical selection is just one aspect of lexicogrammatical selection, or 'wording'", "metaphorical variation is lexicogrammatical rather than simply lexical". Therefore, "there is also such a thing as grammatical metaphor". According to Halliday, "there are two main types of grammatical metaphor in the clause: metaphors of mood (including modality) and metaphors of transitivity". In accordance with his model of semantic functions, these are, respectively, "interpersonal metaphors and ideational metaphors"(Halliday, 1994: 343). It is obvious that the two types of grammatical metaphors are not consistent with the three metafunctions of language in systemic-functional grammar. Martin attempts to add the term textual metaphor to Halliday's original model though his theorization is not convincing enough (Yan Shiqing, 2000: 47-48). Fan Wenfang (2001) makes a systematic study of grammatical metaphor.

What glitters to the author is Halliday's definition of metaphor and his perspectives of the relationship between language and metaphor.

Instead of describing metaphor as variation in the use of words, Halliday defines metaphor as "variation in the expression of meaning" (Halliday, 1994: 341, 342). This is in line with Halliday's ideas of language as a stratificational system composing three levels of meaning, lexicogrammar and phonology in the relationship of realization. Meaning is realized by lexicogrammar in different forms, literal/congruent forms or metaphorical/incongruent forms. Of course, the literal realization is confined by the meaning or the reality, being the direct reflection of the reality. The metaphorical realization must be influenced by a human mind. What functions most seems to be the force of metaphor, which causes the generation of metaphorical variation.

Grammatical metaphor also indicates that metaphor is simply a natural extension of the in-built flexibility and multi-functionality of language. “A language element (a word, a grammatical structure, etc.) initially evolves to serve a particular function; but once it exists as part of language, it is available for other recognizably related uses: the use of the word ‘leg’ can be extended to cover part of a table, or the grammatical class of nouns can be extended to cover actions, events and states” (Thompson, 1996: 165). Thus one sentence pattern, SVC, for example, can be used to realize all kinds of processes, as will be discussed in Chapter Three and Chapter Four.

According to Halliday, language is inherently metaphorical. Though meaning is realized in both congruent forms and incongruent forms, “it is possible that metaphoric variation has been inherent in the nature of language from the very beginning”(Halliday, 1994: 343). For example, primitive citizens might first learn to say that *he is an eagle* or *the earth is thirsty.* (The two sentences are definitely metaphorical.) As time goes on, they develop some abstract concepts and rephrase the two sentences as *he is brave* and *the earth is dry.* This shows that metaphor is a factor in the production of sentences.

Halliday also maintains that language development is characterized by its demetaphorization. Though congruent forms and metaphorical forms are in contrast, “there is no very clear line to be drawn between what is congruent and what is incongruent”. “Much of the history of every language is a history of demetaphorizing: of expressions which began as metaphors gradually losing their metaphorical character”(Halliday, 1994: 348). Take the examples *she has brown eyes, he has a broken wrist,* when the congruent forms would be *her eyes are brown, his wrist is broken.* “But ‘these metaphors’ have become part of the system of English; they are now the unmarked [nonmetaphorical] form of encoding for these particular types of process”(Halliday, 1994: 348). Therefore, “the instances of grammatical metaphor are abundant and universal in language use" (Yan Shiqing, 2000: 174). In other words, grammatical metaphor is universal to all human languages. Then why? It is because, as Hu Zhuanglin says, reality is reflected in language in terms of grammatical forms through the process of metaphorization (胡壮麟, 1996: 2).

In a word, "the grammatical metaphor theory is not only a development of the traditional metaphor theory, but also promises a fresh approach to the study of the generation of sentences" (Yan Shiqing, 2000: 173).

1.2.3 Studies on Metaphor in Cognitive Linguistics

In the long history of the study of metaphor, it is the cognitivists who have made a breakthrough. A significant landmark is the publication in 1980 of *Metaphors We Live By* by Lakoff and Johnson. According to the authors, "the essence of metaphor is understanding and experiencing one kind of thing in terms of another" (Lakoff & Johnson, 1980: 5). "Metaphor is pervasive in everyday life, not just in language, but in thought and action. Our ordinary conceptual system, in terms of which we both think and act, is fundamentally metaphorical in nature." Since our conceptual system plays a central role in defining our everyday reality, "the way we think, what we experience, and what we do every day is very much a matter of metaphor"(Lakoff & Johnson, 1980: 3). Lakoff and Johnson divide metaphor into conceptual metaphors or metaphorical concepts and linguistic metaphors or metaphorical expressions. Linguistic metaphors are merely surface manifestations of conceptual metaphors. Conceptual metaphors include structural metaphors, orientational metaphors and ontological metaphors. Lakoff and Johnson also make a distinction between conventional metaphors and novel metaphors. What they are interested in are the conventional metaphors.

What sheds light for the author is the cognitive definition of metaphor, the nature of metaphor, the distinction between conceptual metaphors and linguistic metaphors, and the emphasis on the study of conventional metaphors.

With a harsh criticism of the traditional view of metaphor as "a device of poetic imagination" and "rhetorical flourish"(Lakoff & Johnson, 1980: 3), Lakoff and Johnson offer their cognitive view of metaphor: "the essence of metaphor is understanding and experiencing one kind of thing in terms of another". Metaphor is "characterized by the conceptualization of one cognitive domain in terms of components more usually associated with another cognitive domain"(Taylor, 1989: 132-133). It is "a conceptual mapping from a source domain to a target domain, with both ontological correspondences and epistemic correspondences entailed by the mapping" (Yu Ning, 1998: 15). All these definitions indicate that metaphor should be understood as "metaphorical concept". Metaphor is fundamentally conceptual by nature.

Being conceptual, metaphor allows us to understand one thing in terms of another, mapping a concept from one domain to another. Such mappings involve projections from the source domain to the target domain. Each metaphorical mapping is a fixed set of ontological correspondences between entities in the source domain and entities in the target domain. When these fixed ontological correspondences are activated, mappings can project source domain inference patterns onto target domain inference patterns. If an animal, for example, is metaphorized as a person, it should have the properties of a person. It can speak, think, and have emotions, etc. Another example is the conceptual metaphor TIME IS MONEY. Since we understand time as money, we also talk about time as money. So we can *spend time, waste time* or *save time* just as we do for money. Thus "the concept is metaphorically structured, the activity is metaphorically structured, and, consequently, the language is metaphorically structured"(Lakoff & Johnson, 1980: 5). In other words, metaphor is one of the mechanisms through which we comprehend reality and structure our language. Conceptual metaphors function to produce linguistic metaphors.

Yet the projections of correspondences are partial in that only part of the structure of the source domain is projected onto the target domain. When we view a mountain as a person, we just map the structure of *head, shoulder, waist* and *foot* of people on it. We do not project *arm, leg, hand*, etc., on it. Therefore, not all metaphorical expressions are acceptable. Some are not acceptable though they may be generated by the same conceptual metaphor.

Cognitivists lay more emphasis on the study of conventional metaphors. To them, "the metaphors that have unconsciously been built into the language by long-established conventions are the most important ones" (Ungerer & Schmid, 1996: 119). This metaphor system plays a major role in both grammar and lexicon of a language. Syntactic generation and lexical extension owe a lot to conventional metaphors. Even novel or poetic metaphor is, for the most part, an extension of the conventional system of metaphorical thought, and constrained by the same principle as conventional metaphor. They are generated by the same rules of mapping.

1.3 Working Definition of the Metaphorical Sentence

If the author is right in assuming that metaphorization is a mechanism of generating sentences, sentences can be divided into two groups: metaphorical sentences and nonmetaphorical sentences. Metaphorical sentences are generated by a metaphorical mechanism. Nonmetaphorical sentences are those directly modeled upon the relation of entities in reality. They are both used to express events happening in the outside and inside worlds of human beings.

However, language has the capacity of variability, negotiability and adaptability (Verschuren, 1999: 58-62). A language system is a multiple functional meaning potential. Once a sentence pattern is established, it serves different kinds of purposes. It may be used nonmetaphorically or metaphorically. Think of the sentences (1) and (2) again:

(1) Mary *saw* them at the summit.

(2) <u>The fifth day</u> *saw* them at the summit.

These two sentences are of the same sentence pattern (SVO(A)), but the first is nonmetaphorical while the second is metaphorical.

What is different between the two sentences is the Subject. The former is animate and the latter is inanimate. Of course, animate entities can *see* while inanimate entities cannot. But if we look from another angle, that of the verb, we find that *see* requires an animate Subject. Therefore, if the Subject of *see* is animate, Sentence (2) is congruent. If the Subject is inanimate, Sentence (2) is incongruent.

Look at two other examples:

(5) He *went through* the forest.

(6) He *went through* the phone book.

In these two sentences, the difference lies in the Object. The verbal phrase *go/went through* requires a physical cubic entity such as forest, channel, etc., as its Object. But in Sentence (6), *phone book* is used, which is physical but not cubic. Hence Sentence (6) is metaphorical.

On the basis of the above analysis, we define in this book **the metaphorical sentence as a sentence in which the relationships between the verb on the one hand and the Subject, and/or the Object/Complement on the other are incongruent with or uncorresponding to reality.**

Several points need to be clarified about the definition.

The first point is about the different levels of metaphorical expressions in language. Metaphor exists at different linguistic levels of word, phrase, sentence, and even discourse (Kitty, 1987: 19; Cameron & Low, 1999: 14; Yan Shiqing, 2000: 83-86). Lexical metaphors are abundant and pervasive in language. For example, *stone-deaf, dog-tired, crystal-clear, knee-deep, shoulder-high , knee-cap, childlike, mousy, sheepish, cuboids* in English and *鹅卵石，杏眼，柳眉，鹰鼻，兔唇，罗圈腿，面包车，剑麻，钉子户，处女地，蝶泳，梅花鹿，鸭舌帽，石笋，火舌，雪花，文化沙漠，人造卫星，黄金时代* in Chinese. Metaphors at phrase level are exemplified as *a rain of bullets, a cloud of arrows, a drop in price; wooden face, sunny smile, fertile imagination* in English and *沙漠之舟，人生道路，一线希望，生命之春；苦笑，肥缺，滚烫的话语，*

甜言蜜语，冷嘲热讽 in Chinese. Sentential metaphors are omnipresent in language, of which the most important patterns are *A is B metaphor* or "*xyz metaphor*" (Cameron & Low, 1999: 15). Examples (2), (4) and (6) are all sentential metaphors. Metaphor at the discourse level means that the whole text is a metaphor, such as allegories, fables and parables. As this research is involved in the interpretation of the relation between sentences, sentential metaphors are naturally the focus.

The second point is about the central status of the predicate verb in syntactic structures. What sentence pattern can be used usually depends on the main verb of the sentence, so verbs are the most important element in the choice of sentence patterns (张今、陈云清，1981：24；张今，1990：30；章振邦，1983：19；胡裕树、范晓，1995：1；Quirk et al, 1985: 50). This is indeed in accordance with Halliday (1994), who believes that when we want to express a meaning, we choose the process first. "Process is central, ... and the other elements are defined by their relationship to it: they are participants in, or circumstance for, the process" (Thompson, 1996: 167). Nevertheless, when a linking verb is the predicate verb of a sentence, the most important element is the Complement after the linking verb (张今、陈云清，1981：24).

The third point is about the notion of congruence. This concept is used by Halliday (1994) to define grammatical metaphor, but Halliday fails to provide an explicit definition or a fixed and applicable criterion for it. He just hints that "the congruent forms" are "the typical way in which experience is construed". He continues to argue that "knowing what are the typical ways of saying things is part of knowing a language". However, he is not so sure about what is typical. He states that "the typical might be the way one first learns to say something in one's mother tongue, or the way it is most commonly said, or the way it is said in the absence of any special circumstances; and these will not coincide". Nevertheless, he insists that "there are what speakers recognize as typical patterns of wording, and it is these that we are calling 'congruent' forms" (Halliday, 1994: 343).

Many practitioners in functional linguistics find this a defect of the Hallidayan theorization. They try to define the term so as to make contributions to the grammatical metaphor theory. Thompson claims that "the term congruent can be informally glossed as 'closer to the state of affairs in the external world'". "In simple terms, nouns congruently encode things, and verbs congruently encode happenings." (Thompson, 1996: 164-165) Yan Shiqing, from the perspective of cognitive linguistics, states that "congruent forms ... are isomorphous with the optimal instances of the prototypes" (Yan Shiqing, 2000: 186). Fan Wenfang provides a different definition to both the congruent and the incongruent. "By congruent realization, we mean that ... the relation between semantic and grammatical categories is natural." "In contrast, incongruent realization refers to the relation between semantic and grammatical categories which is unnatural." (Fan Wenfang, 2001: 30) She is also correct to point out that "grammatical categories should not be confined to grammatical word classes only". "They include other grammatical categories such as mood and modality." (Fan Wenfang, 2001: 30) They naturally consist of sentence patterns.

Congruence, in this book, means that grammatical categories in language are correspondent with semantic categories in reality. For example, entities are depicted as nouns, happenings are described as verbs, attributes are expressed as adjectives, and circumstances are represented as adverbs and prepositional phrases. Further, people are described in language as doing what they can do in reality. They have the attributes and properties they can have in reality. Similarly, animals, plants, and entities, abstract or physical, are interpreted to be what they can be in the real world. Thus the relationship between grammatical categories is correspondent with the relationship between the entities in the real world.

The fourth point is about the incongruent relationships between the predicate verb and other elements in metaphorical sentences. The incongruent relationships may occur between the predicate verb and the Subject (as in (2)), and the predicate verb and the Object (as in (6)). They can also happen between the Subject, the predicate verb and the Object/Complement. For example:

(7) A sudden shower *killed* the wind.

(8) Tom *is* a lion.

While the predicate verb *kill* requires both an animate Subject and an animate Object, neither is animate in sentence (7). This metaphorical sentence is represented by the incongruent relationships between both the predicate verb and the Subject, and the predicate verb and the Object. Therefore, it is represented by the incongruent relationships between the Subject, the predicate verb and the Object.

Similarly, *is* in (8) is used to link the Subject and the Complement. It requires that the Subject and the Complement should be of the same category or that the Complement is the appropriate attribute of the Subject. However, (8) does not meet these requirements. While the Subject is human, the Complement is non-human. Therefore, this metaphorical sentence is represented by the incongruent relationship between the Subject, the verb and the

Complement.

Fifthly, metaphorical sentences are linguistic metaphors. They are linguistic realizations and manifestations of conceptual metaphors. Only after an entity is conceptualized metaphorically as another can it be expressed metaphorically as another in language. For example, conceptually the abstract entity *idea* is considered as a physical object, or more specifically, goods, so we can talk about *having, getting, borrowing* or even *selling ideas*; something or someone can *give us ideas*, we can *put ideas somewhere*, for example, *into other people's heads* (Ungerer & Schmid, 1996: 125).

Finally, metaphorical sentences are not new kinds of sentences in grammar. They are just examined from a new perspective of the dynamic changes in sentence patterns. They are only new types of sentences derived from the basic sentence patterns. The study of metaphorical sentences sheds new light on the relationship between the two kinds of sentences.

1.4 Framework of the Book

1.4.1 General Aims of the Book

The primary objective of this book is to make more comprehensive and more explicative the theory of the generation of sentence patterns advanced by Zhang Jin to better explain the relationship between sentences. It is an extension and elaboration of Zhang Jin's theory. On the basis of the previous studies on metaphor, the author suggests that metaphorization be one of the generative mechanisms of sentences. Thus the whole structure of Zhang Jin's theory of the generation of sentence patterns should include the generation of the basic sentence patterns directly from reality and the other four generative mechanisms of combination, substitution, transformation and metaphorization from the basic sentence patterns. Specifically, the current research is designed to make a tentative study of metaphorical sentences in English and Chinese. It focuses on the generation and the representation of metaphorical sentences in the two languages.

1.4.2 Theoretical Background

The present work is conducted generally in line with the theory of relation between language, reality and thought in Marxist philosophy, which holds that reality determines language and language is the reflection of reality. Language reflects reality actively through the human mind, so language may reflect reality congruently or incongruently. The congruent reflection is nonmetaphorical while the incongruent realization is metaphorical.

Another theory which the author has profited by is Zhang Jin's theory of prototype and model (张今, 1997: 6-9) which includes six main points. 1) All entities, including matter, consciousness, action, nature, society, science, art, etc., are characterized ontologically by mould or pattern. 2) All entities develop their feature, quality, shape and appearance by modeling again and again on their prototypes. 3) Different things are produced either because the same model patterns on different prototypes or because different models pattern on the same prototype. 4) The process from the prototype to the model is an embryologically generative process. 5) The basic principle of the theory is that models are patterned on prototypes on the basis of resemblance. 6) Language is modeled on reality by human beings on purpose so as to know the world, to change the world and to preserve humans themselves. In the view of this theory, the objective material and mental world is the prototype while language and speech are the models that imitate and reflect the former. Reality is the content of cognition and language is the form of cognition. Though the content is the same, the form may be different because models are made by people who are strongly influenced by their attitudes about nature and society as well as their experiences, interests, cultural background, etc.

In addition, the author also owes a lot to the theories of modern linguistics, especially cognitive linguistics and systemic functional linguistics.

Cognitive linguistics accounts for the relationship between language and reality by resorting to the human cognitive mechanism, laying stress on the interaction of reality, language and cognition. It "posits an intimate, dialectic relationship between the structure and function of language on the one hand, and nonlinguistic skills and knowledge on the other hand"(Taylor, 1989: viii). It believes that natural language is a product of the human mind, based on the same organizing principles that operate in other cognitive domains. Language structure depends on (and influences) conceptualization, the latter being conditioned by our experience of ourselves, the external world, and our relation to that world. In other words, language is not just a system consisting of arbitrary signs, but its structures are related to and motivated by human conceptual knowledge. It is "motivated by a number of factors — by actually existing discontinuities in the world, by the manner in which human beings interact, in a given culture, with the world, and by general cognitive processes of concept formation" (Taylor, 1989: vii-viii).

Among cognitive theories, Lakoff and Johnson's conceptual metaphor theory sheds much light on this study. Lakoff and Johnson draw an important distinction between conceptual metaphors and linguistic metaphors. Metaphorical language, consisting of specific linguistic expressions, is but a surface manifestation or realization of conceptual metaphor.

The systemic functionalists prove that language has three metafunctions, of which ideational metafunction is about the relationship between language and reality. This metafunction is realized by the transitivity system, either congruently or incongruently. The incongruent realization is a grammatical metaphor.

Though the theories mentioned above are of different schools, they are consistent with each other in one aspect, that they all offer a dialectic view on language which allows the interaction between language, reality and cognition. Therefore, the book is cognition-oriented.

It has been assumed that the world man lives in can be categorized into physical and abstract entities. The former can be further divided into two categories: animate things and inanimate things. Animate things include animals and plants while animals can be again classified into lower animals (normal use of "animal") and higher animals (human beings).

According to cognitive sciences, the development of human cognition is, as a rule, from the tangible physical entities to the intangible and abstract entities and then to the nonentities. So people are inclined to model abstract things on physical things. People understand abstract things in terms of physical things through their understandings of human beings, animals, plants and inanimate objects. When they express other things in terms of the physical things mentioned, they make a metaphorical sentence. Thus metaphorical sentences are created by personification, animalization, plantification, hypostatization and alienation.

However, when man gets to know the world, he does it not merely by impressing the names of the separate things on his mind, but by realizing an individual thing's features, behaviour, action and its relation with other things. All these can be typically expressed in a transitivity system of verb processes. The features, for example, can be represented by a relational process, the behaviour by a behavioural process, and the happening by a material process or an abstract entity process. Therefore, when one thing is modeled on another, it also adopts the features, the behaviour and the action of another. One process may express the meaning of different processes. The incongruence of process realization can be represented by Subject-verb transitivity systems, verb-Object transitivity systems, and Subject-verb-Object/Complement transitivity systems.

Though metaphorical sentences in English and Chinese are generated via the same mechanisms of personification, animalization, plantification, hypostatization and alienation, and represented by the same transitivity systems between Subject-verb relationships, verb-Object relationships, and Subject-verb-Object/Complement relationships, some differences between English metaphorical sentences and Chinese metaphorical sentences have been found by the author. Such differences can be illustrated through E-C translation.

1.4.3 Composition of the Book

The book falls into six parts. In addition to the ongoing introductory part (Chapter One), Chapter Two is about the generative mechanisms of metaphorical sentences in English and Chinese. The representation of metaphorical sentences in the two languages is discussed in Chapter Three and Chapter Four. Chapter Five focuses on the translation of English metaphorical sentences into Chinese. Chapter Six is the conclusion.

1.4.4 Data

The data for the present research includes new interpretations of used data in relevant studies as well as fresh data drawn from various sources, including textbooks, newspapers, magazines, dictionaries, etc. However, the actual sources of the data such as the page and the date of the newspaper are not recorded, on purpose, mainly because some of the examples have to be simplified so as to keep them short and concise. In so doing, the examples are made simpler and more to the point. Therefore, not all the examples are "original" as they are in the original version. But the abridgments have not changed their metaphorical structure. Furthermore, they are still good and natural English and Chinese to the native speakers. Some examples, mainly from dictionaries, are highly conventionalized and idiomatic expressions.

Chapter Two

Generative Mechanisms of Metaphorical Sentences in English and Chinese

2.1 Introductory Remarks

The investigation into the mechanisms of metaphor is usually initiated with efforts to structure metaphor, i.e., to establish the constituent parts of metaphor, such as Richards' distinction between tenor and vehicle (束定芳, 2000b: 154), Black's focus and frame, primary subject and secondary subject, principal subject and subsidiary subject (束定芳, 2000b: 163), Taylor's donor domain and receptor domain (Taylor, 1989: 132), Cameron's Topic domain and Vehicle domain (Cameron & Low, 1999: 19), or Lakoff & Johnson's source domain and target domain (Lakoff & Johnson, 1980). The benefit of such an approach consists in the facilities it can offer to construct rules governing the operations of metaphor with the identification of contrastive pairs. Following Lakoff and Johnson, the author will categorize metaphor as mapping from the source domain to the target domain, or in terms of Professor Zhang Jin's prototype and model theory, from prototype to model, on the basis of resemblance. Therefore, **prototypes and source domains, models and target domains are used synonymously in this book**.

2.2 Generative Mechanisms of Metaphorical Sentences

2.2.1 The Role of Cognition in Metaphor Creation

The conceptual nature of metaphor suggests that the mechanism of metaphor is much related to human cognition and ultimately the kind of culture that a language represents.

To cognitive linguists, language is not just a system, consisting of arbitrary signs, and its structures are related to and motivated by human conceptual knowledge. Language is inseparable from conceptual thought, while conceptual thought is inseparable from human experience. Human cognition plays a very important role in the structuring of language. Usually, language is congruent with reality. So nouns are used to realize entities, verbs are used to realize processes, and adverbs or prepositional phrases are used to realize the circumstantial elements. In language people are supposed to do, to speak, to think, to feel, to behave as people really do in reality.

Entities are supposed to be or to exist as they do in the material world. But language does not act in this easy way. Instead, it may work more complicatedly. Entities can do things as people do, people can do many things as entities do. Even nonentities can do like entities.

There are two reasons for the above phenomenon, both concerning cognition of the human mind. One is that the human mind limits their knowledge about the outside and the inside world. People sometimes do not know how to express their experience about the world. They have to rely on the knowledge they already have. They have to model what they do not know on what they know. That is the designatory function of metaphor. This designatory metaphor involves giving names to new or nameless things or giving an expression to a new phenomenon. It applies to both lexicon and grammar. The application in lexicon can be exemplified in word formation and lexical semantic extension as discussed in 1.2.1 and 1.3. More examples are the American toponyms that are named after places in the Old World such as *New York*, *New Jersey*, *New Haven*. It is clear that these names are in fact brought into being by modeling upon old ones and so are the products of designatory metaphors. A similar case is that in many languages the names of sea animals are only those of the land animals slightly elaborated (preceded by *sea* or *海* to indicate the classification), as *sea lion, sea snake, sea horse* in English and *海豹, 海狮, 海狗, 海马* in Chinese. "Here, it is obvious that human beings take advantage of ready-made signs for land animals and designate the sea animals accordingly" (Yang Lili, 1997: 34).

The application of designatory metaphor in grammar can be exemplified in metaphorical expressions of abstract concepts, such as emotion and time. The emotion of anger is usually expressed in terms of heat or internal pressure while the emotion of happiness is often expressed in the metaphors of orientation and light (Yu Ning, 1998: 4). Therefore, in Chinese anger is described as *生气* (produce gas) while happiness is described as *高兴* (high-spirit). Similarly, notions of time are expressed in terms of space, thus saying *long time, remote time, short time* in English and *时间长，时间短* in Chinese.

The other reason for the noncorresponding relationship between language and reality is that the human mind plays an active part in the cognition of the outside and inside worlds. Instead of using the normal literal way to express reality, people use figurative expressions, which are more colourful, more vivid and more effective. Such is the substitutional function of metaphor. This substitutional metaphor involves a different expression of a given meaning. For example, instead of saying *Mary saw a wonderful sight*, or *A great many people protested*, people may metaphorically say *A wonderful sight met Mary's eyes*, or *Protests flooded in.*

"Viewing metaphor as substitution is quite an ancient affair which can be traced back at least to Aristotle and which has been accepted part and parcel by traditional rhetoricians" (Yang Lili, 1997: 33). According to this point of view, metaphor is a way of substitution for platitudinous expressions to achieve rhetorical and poetic value. This long-held point of view dominates the history of metaphor studies. Therefore, it is natural that metaphor has been taken as an exclusive domain for rhetoricians and literary critics.

It is true that most poetic metaphors are metaphors of substitution. Many metaphors are substitutional. However, designatory metaphor is as important as the substitutional in language, if not more important. First of all, it is a very important way for man to structure the outside world, and man's structuring of the outside world is an important step in his understanding and changing of the world. Second, it is an efficient way to model new experience on the old through recategorization and restructuring. Consequently, man's knowledge about the world accumulates day by day, but words and grammatical structures need not increase simultaneously. Third, designatory metaphor characterizes the nature of language. It is mainly because of this kind of metaphor that Lakoff and Johnson (Lakoff & Johnson, 1980:5) claim that language is metaphorical by nature. Without this sort of metaphor, a language would be totally inconceivable.

Though metaphor can be classified into substitutional and designatory, the classification is not something clearcut. In the treatment of a particular instance, it is harmful to be absolute and arbitrary, since there are instances which have changed from one kind to the other. For example, the sentences *The earth is thirsty* and *He is an eagle*, which are used by primitives, are originally metaphors of designation, since they are the only ways the primitives can represent the phenomenon. But as time goes on, our ancestors develop some abstract concepts and rephrase the two sentences as *The earth is dry* and *He is brave*. The original two sentences are no longer designatory metaphors. They become metaphors of substitution instead, because there are now more logical, more straightforward, more literal, more congruent ways to represent the phenomenon.

In conclusion, cognition functions in two ways in the creation of metaphor. One is the passive limitations of human cognition in understanding the world while the other is the active participation in the recategorization and restructuring of the world. Though they are different, they both involve understanding one thing in terms of another, which is a very important factor in the mechanism of metaphor creation.

2.2.2 The Role of Resemblance in Metaphor Creation

As discussed above, cognition enables man to understand one thing in terms of another. Things of different kinds, different natures, with different images can be recast into a metaphor. But what enables cognition to map one thing onto another? What are the grounds for the cross-domain mappings? Or simply, why could one thing be considered as another? The answer is that the two things in a metaphor share resemblance or similarity.

According to the principle of similarity, "individual elements that are similar tend to be perceived as one common segment" (Ungerer & Schmid, 1996: 33). Among similars "what is true of one is also true of the rest" (Kitty, 1987: 3). Resemblance between the two constituents of a metaphor permits human beings to conceptualize one thing in terms of the other.

Resemblance, in this book, is used in its broad sense. It does not only mean the objective and physical resemblance in shape and function, as exemplified in the phrases *the mouth of a river*, *the foot of a mountain*. It also consists of mental and experiential resemblances, such as "sensational resemblance", "perceptual resemblance", "conceptual resemblance" and "imaginary resemblance" (Yang Lili, 1997: 23). Mental resemblance is based on psychological perception and bodily experience. For instance, *I'm feeling up* and *I'm feeling down* are expressions of happiness and sadness in English. They are based on the bodily experience that one would keep his body straight and upward when happy but droop and bend his body when sad.

Though all these types of resemblance supply the necessary nutrients for the growth of metaphor, it is man's metaphorical thinking that establishes the relation of resemblance between two things by means of imagination. Therefore, imaginary resemblance is the most important of all. Imaginary resemblance involves the resemblance discovered by imaginary thinking and the resemblance created in imaginary thinking. Hence there is also such a thing as creative resemblance (束定芳, 2000b: 173). Once the relation of resemblance between two things is established, one thing, the model, can act as the other, the prototype. It can behave, function as the other, and wear the appearance of the other, bear the features of the other. For example, if *anger* can be understood and considered to be fire, flood, storm, ice, beast, etc., it can be expressed as if it *burns*, *flames*, *boils*, *melts*, *congeals*, *falls*, *rises*, *bursts out*, *roars*, *dies*, etc., and can be featured as being *hot*, *cold*, *white, icy, kindling, blazing, scorching, smouldering, devouring, cyclonic, seething*, etc. (Yang Lili, 1997: 20).

A special type of resemblance is contiguity. Contiguity means "being together" (Ungerer & Schmid, 1996: 78) or "nearness or neighbourhood" (Ibid: 115). It is synonymous to co-occurrence or proximity, etc. "By definition it signifies the approximation between things in temporal sequence, spatial location and causal relation" (Yang Lili, 1997: 25-26). It is traditionally regarded as the essential element of metonymy and synecdoche. As metaphor is created on the basis of resemblance, so synecdoche and metonymy are created on that of contiguity, for example, *White House* for the American president, *Ottawa* for the Canadian government and *Sandwich* for the food Lord Sandwich invented.

Many modern linguists make no distinction between metaphor,

synecdoche and metonymy, taking in such a case the metaphor as the primacy. The author is also fully aware that metaphor and metonymy (including synecdoche) are closely connected because resemblance and contiguity share a very close psychological origin. In other words, in this book what we call metaphor is in its broad sense and includes synecdoche and metonymy as well.

Everything man senses or perceives occurs in particular temporal and spatial dimensions. When man at the same time and in the same space senses and perceives a mass of thing (even if the mass later on turns out to be two or more different things), he may project this temporal and spatial sameness onto the thing and regard it as a whole. Therefore, in psychological origin, the relation of contiguity is also established by resemblance, resemblance of time and space in sensation and perception.

There are many examples to support this assumption. Actually, almost all of the conceptual metaphors by Lakoff and Johnson are generated on the basis of contiguity. Yu Ning even generalizes "a metonymic principle" (Yu Ning, 1998: 51, 56, 63) that the physiological effects of an emotion stand for the emotion. With this principle, the emotion of *anger* can be understood in both English and Chinese as *body heat, internal pressure, redness in face and neck area, agitation and interference with accurate perception*. Consider the conceptual metaphor MORE IS UP. As you add objects to a pile, the pile gets higher. This experience establishes a natural association between quantity and vertical extent. This association is one of metonymy. Therefore, Taylor draws a conclusion that these metaphors are "grounded, ultimately, in metonymy" (Taylor, 1989: 139).

Another type of similarity is analogy which means the

resemblance, not of the two things themselves, but of two or more attributes, circumstances, or effects. If two things bear an analogous relationship to each other, the analogy can be a basis for a metaphor. One example is *He sleeps forever in the grave*, which indicates the resemblance between the state of sleep and the state of death. Another example is *The sea smiled at him*, which points out the analogous relationship between *man* and *smile* versus *sea* and *shine*.

Before we put an end to this section, two points must be made clear. One is that resemblance is a matter of degree (束定芳, 2000b: 177; Yan Shiqing, 2000: 91; Taylor, 1989: 60). Things may be more similar, or less similar. Generally speaking, things of the same category are more similar while those of different classes are less similar. But since metaphor involves understanding one thing in terms of another, the resemblance between the two components in a metaphor is very different in nature from the similitude between two things of the same kind. The critical point in creating a metaphor is to find similarity in diversity. For example, in the metaphorical sentence *A good man is a square*, a good man and a square are obviously different categories of different classes. They do not share any similarities in shape or function, but they are conceptualized similarly because they are both perfect. Therefore, there is no such thing as more similar things being more likely connected, or less similar things being less likely linked, in a metaphor.

Similarity may also be a subjective notion which has no foundation in reality. Such similarity, like beauty, lies in the eye of the beholder. Things may be "similar to the extent that a human being, in some context or for some purpose, chooses to regard them as similar" (Taylor, 1989: 60). This might explain why some metaphors are available only to some people. It is to these people that the metaphorical constituents are similar. Of course, these metaphors may induce other people to find the resemblance and thus become popular. If other people cannot sense the resemblance, the metaphor will vanish from language.

2.2.3 Source Domain and Target Domain in Metaphor Creation

As metaphor is a conceptual mapping from the source domain to the target domain, it seems reasonable to ask what typical source domains and what typical target domains are. The cognitive answer is that the source domains are typically concrete and physical while the target domains are typically abstract and nonphysical since human conceptual systems "contain mappings of inference patterns from typically more concrete domains to typically more abstract domains" (Yu Ning, 1998: 22). As a basic cognitive structure, metaphor allows us to understand relatively abstract or inherently unstructured subject matter in terms of a more concrete, or at least a more highly structured subject matter. In fact, many subject matters such as time and emotion can only be comprehended via metaphor. In short, metaphor is the main mechanism through which we comprehend abstract concepts and perform abstract reasoning.

"To function as a source domain for a metaphor, a domain must be understood independent of metaphor." (Lakoff, 1987: 276) It must be something concrete and physical about which man can develop knowledge directly on the basis of his bodily experience. Therefore, for our conceptualization of abstract categories we rely on the basic experiences of the general classes of objects, organisms and persons. This object/organism/person view of the world facilitates the cognitive handling and manipulating of abstract categories. Thus many abstract concepts are comprehended as objects, animate entities or human beings such as the conceptual metaphors IDEAS ARE OBJECTS, IDEAS ARE ANIMATE BEINGS OR PERSONS. The reason we can understand abstract categories in terms of these general classes is that the specific way we interact with instances of the three classes is extremely familiar to us, and this interaction provides the source for the metaphorical mappings.

While source domains are usually those concrete, physical and tangible categories comprehended directly on the basis of bodily experience, target domains are often those abstract, nonphysical and intangible categories that are not easy to understand directly. Among the target domains are anger, hate, happiness, love, lust, argument, communication, ideas, theories, life, death, quantity, authority, power, evaluation, social structure, event structure, etc.

From the discussion above, we can see that cognitive linguists confirm the directionality of metaphorical transfer from concrete source domains to abstract target domains. "Such mappings are asymmetric in that they are one-directional, involving projections from a source domain to a target domain." (Yu Ning, 1998: 32-33) They are unidirectional because bodily experience of the concrete categories serves as the source of our understanding of the abstract ones, but not the other way round. Nevertheless, many examples show that both the source domain and the target domain can be concrete and physical. In other words, metaphorical mappings also involve transference between concrete concepts. This is because metaphor is "a very convenient and economic way of referring to things" (Ungerer & Schmid, 1996: 127). A ready example is the metaphors composed of *butcher* and *surgeon*: *The butcher is a surgeon* or *the surgeon is a butcher*. Of course the two metaphors have quite different senses. Yet what matters to us here is that both butcher and surgeon are concrete concepts and that they can serve as both a source domain and a target domain. Therefore, it is possible for us to understand *butcher* in terms of *surgeon* and also *surgeon* in terms of *butcher*. Though we are familiar with both the terms, the metaphorical mappings help us understand what kind of surgeon one is by means of the knowledge of a butcher, and what kind of a butcher one is by means of the knowledge of a surgeon. If a butcher should act as if he were a surgeon and treat his patient (an animal) like a person, taking too much time and being too tentative as he cuts up a piece of meat, he would be an incompetent butcher. The metaphor is intended and understood as a negative evaluation of the butcher's competence. Casting him as a surgeon highlights the incongruity between his methods and those appropriate to a butcher. Similarly, if a surgeon should act as if he were a butcher and treat his patient (a person) as an animal, working too carelessly, he would be an incompetent surgeon. Again the metaphor is intended and understood as a negative evaluation of a surgeon's competence. Casting him as a butcher highlights the incongruity between his methods and those suitable for a surgeon.

To round off this section, it is necessary to make clear the notion of domain. According to Langacker, a domain is "a context for the characterization of a semantic unit" (Langacker, 1987: 147). Domains are necessarily cognitive entities and cognitive units such as mental experiences and representational spaces. Most concepts are context dependent and at the same time serve to define other concepts, be it implicit or explicit. In other words, most concepts presuppose other concepts and in turn are defined by reference to them. Concepts are mutually dependent. Langacker uses the concept KNUCKLE to illustrate what a domain is. "The concept KNUCKLE ... presupposes the conception of a finger. It would be virtually impossible to explain what a knuckle is without somehow invoking the conception of a finger as a holistic entity." "Given the concept of FINGER, KNUCKLE is easily and straightforwardly characterized. FINGER provides the necessary context—or domain—for the characterization of KNUCKLE."(Langacker, 1987: 147-148) But FINGER is not itself a primitive notion. It is similarly characterized in part by its position relative to a HAND, HAND in relation to an ARM, and ARM in relation to the BODY as a whole. Therefore, it is natural for most concepts to be understood as domains. Thus the author is free to use other terms such as concepts, categories, models and even items or things instead of domains throughout the book.

Although it is typical for one concept to serve as a domain for the characterization of another, there must be a point of which no further reduction is possible. So far as shape is concerned, the notion BODY is a configuration in three-dimensional space which is a concept not definable relative to some other, more fundamental conception. This sort of primitive representational field is referred to as a basic domain. Any non-basic domain is called a subdomain.

Though a basic domain cannot be described in terms of more fundamental concepts, the field of conceptual potential it defines may nevertheless be structured. The concepts it permits can be ordered or grouped in various ways and be determined to lie at different "distances" from one another, and the domain can be described in terms of one or more dimensions.

2.2.4 Generative Mechanisms of Metaphorical Sentences

As discussed above, metaphor is generated by mapping a source domain concept onto a target domain concept on the basis of resemblance, so a metaphorical sentence, as one form of metaphor, is also generated by mapping concepts from a source domain to a target domain. The mapping direction is usually from the concrete and physical to the abstract and nonphysical. Therefore, the source domain is always concrete while the target domain can be either abstract or concrete. Consequently, the general generative mechanism of metaphorical sentences is concretization. But the specific mechanisms to create metaphorical sentences are personification, animalization, plantification, hypostatization and alienation since concrete things can be further divided. They can be divided into two categories: animate things and inanimate things. Animate things include animals and plants while animals can be again classified into lower animals (normal use of "animal") and higher animals (human beings). If the source domain is a person, a metaphor is generated via personification no matter what the target domain is. It is the same with animalization, plantification and hypostatization. Alienation involves cross-domain mappings between two concrete concepts from one kind of physical entity to another no matter what it is. These mechanisms will be discussed in detail in the following two sections.

2.3 Generative Mechanisms of Metaphorical Sentences in English

This section will deal with the generative mechanisms of metaphorical sentences in English. They are personification, animalization, plantification, hypostatization and alienation.

2.3.1 Personification

Metaphorical sentences in English are usually generated by personification because human beings find it easy to understand things in terms of themselves. They know themselves better than other things in the world. Almost all other things—animals, plants, objects and abstracts—can be modeled on human beings. Even the non-things such as states and facts are also comprehended as human beings. In other words, man and his actions, behaviours, mental and verbal activities supply the main source domains for other non-human, non-object entities. Metaphors generated via personification are called "humanizing metaphors" (Ungerer & Schmid, 1996: 115) or "personification metaphors" (Lakoff & Johnson, 1980: 61; Cameron & Low, 1999: 247, 248).

2.3.1.1 Animals Personified

Animals are the closest neighbours of human beings. They are easily assimilated with humans, understood as humans and hence expressed as humans. When animals are modeled on human beings, the features, behaviours and actions of human beings are projected onto the animals. For example:

(1) The crow *thinks* her own birds fairest.
(2) A female baboon climbed a shrub and *pirated* a nest of eggs.
(3) The bird *sang to welcome* the smiling year.

In all the three examples, animal actions are modeled on those of humans since the animals are modeled on human beings. They are personified. *Think, pirate, sing* and *welcome* are typically used to express actions done by people. They usually require human Subjects. Now they are used with animal Subjects. The animals —*the crow, the female baboon* and *the bird* —are understood as humans and described as humans.

Actually, most animal-toward-human mappings are the norms of language. Sometimes it is difficult to point out their congruent forms. For instance, we have no other choice if we do not say *the crow thinks* ... These metaphors are exactly metaphors of designation. They are the only forms in language to encode man's experience of some phenomena.

2.3.1.2 Plants Personified

Plants also take human beings as their prototypes. Many human features, actions and behaviours can be mapped on plants. For example:

(4) Some trees *give* us fruit; others *give* us wood for building.
(5) The thirsty plants *drank* up the water I gave them.
(6) The evergreen shrubs *struggled* to survive the dust and fumes from a busy main road.

In the three examples above, plants are considered as human

beings. Since they are personified, they adopt human features and actions. Therefore, *trees* in (4) can *give* us things as if they do so on purpose, *plants* (which are *thirsty* as human beings are) in (5) can *drink* though they do not have mouths, and *the evergreen shrubs* in (6) sensitively *struggle* to survive.

2.3.1.3 Objects Personified

Inanimate objects are usually specified as being persons. This allows us to comprehend a wide variety of experiences with nonhuman entities in terms of human motivations, characteristics, and activities. Here are some examples:

(7) The satchel and the hat *wandered* into the darkest corner of the huge wardrobe.

(8) The clock seemed to *refuse* to strike twelve.

(9) The empty house *was longing for* the children to return.

(10) My watch *says* half past ten.

In each of these cases we are seeing something nonhuman as human. In (7), since *the satchel and the hat* are understood as human beings, they can *wander* into the darkest corner of the huge wardrobe. Similarly, in (8) and (9), *the clock* and *the empty house* are experienced as persons, so they can perform such human activities as to *refuse* to do something and *long for* something. In (10), *my watch* is personified, so it can *say* what time it is.

2.3.1.4 Abstracts Personified

Since the basic framework of language was established long before man developed the power of abstraction, in the representation of abstract notions, man conveniently sought the help of the ready-made patterns of actions and behaviour of man himself. In essence, man takes human beings as the source domain and models the non-spatial, the non-tactile and even the incomprehensible upon humans. Here are some examples:

(11) Fortune *is smiling* on us.
(12) Death *robbed* him of his life.
(13) Those ideas *died off* in the Middle Ages.
(14) The next two centuries *witnessed* a great renaissance in all learning.
(15) Necessity is *the mother* of invention.
(16) A trembling *seized* him, and his limbs bent as if for a spring.

In these examples, the abstract concepts are all considered as human beings, therefore, *fortune* can *smile*, *death* can *rob*, *ideas* can *die off*, *centuries* can *witness*, *necessity* can be *the mother* and *a trembling* can *seize*.

2.3.1.5 Facts and Events Personified

In English, facts and events are usually expressed with clauses, finite or nonfinite. A finite clause is a clause whose verbal operator indicates either tense or modality. A nonfinite clause is one whose verb element is nonfinite. These clauses can be nominalized and embedded in other clauses via concretization. The nominal finite clauses are that-clauses and wh-clauses. The nominalized nonfinite clauses are to-infinitives and -ing participles. Personification is one form of concretization. When facts and events are personified, they adopt human features and actions. This will be evidenced by the following examples:

(17) Thinking about her always *gives* me a lift.

(18) It *pays* to be honest.

(19) What you did *helps* enormously.

In (17) and (18), the events expressed by the nonfinite clauses of the -ing participle and the to-infinitive are experienced as humans, so the former can *give* somebody a lift and the latter can *pay*. In (19), the fact expressed by a what-clause is regarded as a person, which *helps* enormously. What should be noted is that the to-infinitive does not appear at the beginning of the sentence. Instead, the formal Subject "it" is put at the beginning. It is usually the same when a that-clause functions as the Subject of a sentence.

In English, facts and events can also be encoded in a nominalization. The nominalized nouns can be regarded as packed clauses because they have "a systematic correspondence with a clause structure" (Quirk, et al, 1985: 1288). These noun phrases, abstract by nature, are always mentally understood as concrete objects. They are sometimes understood as human beings and thus encoded as such. When they are expressed in the linguistic norms of human behaviour and action, a metaphorical sentence emerges. For example:

(20) The beauty of the Saxon women *filled* all England with a new delight and grace.

(21) His failure *suggests* his carelessness.

(22) Stylistic analysis of a text *allows* us to do a similar kind of thing—to examine the workings of a text.

In (20), *the beauty of the Saxon women* is modeled on a person, so it can *fill* all England with a new delight and grace. Similarly, *his failure* in (21) is personified, so that it can *suggest*. In (22) what is personified is *stylistic analysis of a text*, thus it *allows* us to do something.

2.3.2 Animalization

Animals are human cousins that inhabit the same world, share the same sunshine and breeze with man. They have many physical similarities and assumed resemblances with man. They also supply people with the earliest established experiences and thus often serve as the source domains of metaphorical mappings. In other words, non-animal, non-spatial abstracts are often metaphorized as animals.

2.3.2.1 Human Beings Animalized

As mentioned above, man and his animal cousins share many physical similarities and assumed resemblances, it is very convenient to make mutual mappings between man and animal. Animal-toward-human mappings are personification, which has been discussed in 2.3.1.1. Human-toward-animal mappings are animalization. Look at the following examples:

(23) The child *flew* into a rage and began scattering its toys about.
(24) The girl *fluttered* away.
(25) John *hatched* a clever scheme.

In the examples above, people are considered as animals and described as animals. *The child* in (23) is modeled on a bird, so is *the girl* in (24). In (25), *John* is experienced as a hen, which can hatch eggs into chickens. Of course, this sentence also involves a metaphorical mapping of the Object from a physical entity, an egg or a chicken, to an abstract notion, a clever scheme.

2.3.2.2 Plants Animalized

Plants can also be regarded as animals and thus adopt animal actions, behaviours and features. Here are some examples:

(26) Cinchona trees *climbed* higher and higher up the mountain.
(27) Leaves *flutter* past the window.
(28) Dead leaves *were flying* about.

Each of the sentences above involves considering plants as animals. *The cinchona trees* in (26) are patterned on animals which can climb, such as monkeys. *The leaves* or *the dead leaves* in (27) and (28) are modeled on birds, so they can *flutter* and *fly*.

2.3.2.3 Objects Animalized

Inanimate objects often take animals as their prototypes and source domains. They are animalized in the following examples:

(29) The long road *climbed* the hills.
(30) The river *snaked* its way through the jungle.
(31) The yellow fog *rubs its back* on the window panes.
(32) I looked up; a pale glimmer of moonbeams had *alighted* on the summit of the spyglass.

In these sentences, inanimate objects are modeled on animals. *The long road* in (29) is considered as an animal and hence can *climb* the hills. *The river* in (30) is metaphorized as a snake and *the yellow fog* in (31) is thought of as a cat, which often rubs its back upon other things. In (32) *a pale glimmer of moonbeams* is modeled on a bird, so it can *alight* on the summit of the spyglass.

2.3.2.4 Abstracts Animalized

As discussed above, abstract notions are concretized when one refers to them or talks about them. They are supposed to be existing. Animalization is one type of concretization and naturally applies to abstracts. For instance:

(33) Prices *are climbing* day by day.
(34) Pleasant hours *fly* fast.
(35) Cold chills of fear *crept* over me.

Abstract notions in the above sentences are animalized. *Prices* in (33) and *cold chills of fear* in (35) are considered as animals that can *climb* and *creep*. *Pleasant hours* in (34) are experienced as birds, so that they can *fly fast*.

2.3.3 Plantification

Compared with personification and animalization, plantification is not a major mechanism to generate metaphorical sentences in English. However, as one type of animate objects in the world, plants conveniently help people understand other things. In other words, plants function as the source domains. The knowledge of plants is projected on things other than plants.

2.3.3.1 Human Beings Plantified

Though people know themselves very well on the basis of their own experiences, they find it a convenient way to conceive and describe themselves in terms of plants. For instance:

(36) Jack *wilted* under the pressure.

(37) This will make it more difficult to *weed out* people unsuitable for the profession.

(38) He always *cultivates* those people who will be useful to him.

(39) He had a powerful *trunk* but thin arms.

In the examples above, human beings are understood as plants and therefore expressed as plants. They can *wilt*, *be weeded out*, *be cultivated* and *have a trunk* as if they are grass or trees.

2.3.3.2 Objects Plantified

Inanimate objects can take plants as their prototypes and model on them. Thus they adopt the features and behaviours of plants. Consider the following examples:

(40) The road *branches* here.

(41) He *weeded out* one by one the books he didn't want.

(42) That remote barren land *has blossomed* into rich granaries.

In each of the examples above, tangible objects are metaphorized as plants. *The road* in (40) is experienced as a tree, so it can *branch*. In (41) *the books* (he didn't want) are considered as weeds and *are weeded out* one by one. *That remote barren land* in (42) is thought of as flowers, thus it *blossoms*.

2.3.3.3 Abstracts Plantified

Abstract notions can only be concretized when they are expressed in language. It is natural for people to plantify abstracts since plants are easier to conceive and understand. For example:

(43) His knowledge is the *fruit* of long study.

(44) A good teacher *plants* the love of learning in students.

(45) Another equally outstanding design *was germinating* at Bristol.

(46) My hopes *withered* away with the years.

Each of the examples above involves mapping the concept of plants on the abstract concepts. In (43), *his knowledge* is experienced as *fruit. The love of learning* in (44) is considered as seeds, so is *another equally outstanding design* in (45). In (46), *My hopes* are understood as plants in general, so they can *wither away* with the years.

2.3.4 Hypostatization

Hypostatization is the mechanism of viewing non-objects as objects. The source domain is the inanimate substance. As objects are physical and tangible, they are easy to conceive and understand. They are also easy to signify, quantify and modify. Therefore, many other things in cognition and in language can be modeled on objects. They are experienced and expressed as objects.

2.3.4.1 Human Beings Hypostatized

Animate things may transfer toward the source domain of the inanimate substance. The following examples show that human beings are modeled on objects:

(47) Tom *broke* under the cross examination.

(48) The chairman *ploughed* through the discussion.

(49) She *dropped* her friend.

(50) Over the next week, more victims—men, women, children —*flowed* in.

In (47), *Tom* is thought of as a brittle object, which can *break* into pieces under heavy weight. *The chairman* in (48) is considered as a plough, so that he can *plough* through the discussion, just as the plough does through the land. In (49), *her friend* is understood as a physical object that can *be dropped* onto the ground while in (50), *the victims*—men, women, children—are patterned upon liquids such as water.

2.3.4.2 Abstracts Hypostatized

Abstracts, when they need encoding into language, may be hypostatized. They are experienced as physical entities. They adopt the features and behaviours of the inanimate substances. For instance:

(51) The three people *share* their views and hobbies.

(52) He broke her heart and *stole* her happiness.

(53) We'*re generating* a lot of ideas this week.

(54) My mind *isn't operating*.

The abstract notions, *views*, *hobbies* and *happiness*, in (51) and (52) are modeled on inanimate objects in general, so they can *be shared* and *stolen*. In (53) and (54), the abstract concepts are patterned on specific objects, namely, products and machines.

2.3.5 Alienation

As mentioned above, alienation is a mechanism of mapping one kind of concrete thing onto another. It may occur between any kind of concrete things, from a kind of person to another, from a kind of animal to another, from a kind of plant to another, or from a kind of object to another. However, alienation in English only involves mapping from a kind of person to another and mapping from a kind of physical object to another. Alienation of mapping from one kind of person to another may be exemplified by the examples *The surgeon is a butcher* and *The butcher is a surgeon.* Alienation of mapping one kind of object onto another is evidenced as follows:

(55) The machine *is broken* and must be repaired.
(56) The ship *ploughs* the sea.
(57) The cars *flowed* in a steady stream along the main road.

In all the three sentences above, one object is understood as another. *The machine* in (55) is considered as a brittle object which can *be broken.* In (56), *the ship* is regarded as a plough and thus *ploughs* the sea, which is also metaphorized as another object, namely, a piece of land. In (57), *the cars* are experienced as water that flows in a stream steadily.

2.3.6 Summary

This section has presented a study of the generative mechanisms of metaphorical sentences in English. The general mechanism is concretization. Specific mechanisms are personification, animalization, plantification, hypostatization and alienation. Personification is a mechanism of mapping human beings onto other things and animalization involves mapping animals onto other things. Plantification concerns cross-domain mappings from plants to other things. Hypostatization is a mechanism of experiencing nonobjects in terms of objects. Alienation involves understanding one kind of concrete thing in terms of another. Therefore, the generative mechanisms of metaphorical sentences in English can be summarized in Table 1:

Table 1 Generative Mechanisms of Metaphorical Sentences in English

Source / Target	Human Beings	Animals	Plants	Objects	Abstracts	Facts & Events
Human Beings	✔	+	+	+		
Animals	+					
Plants	+	+				
Objects	+	+	+	✔		
Abstracts	+	+	+	+		
Facts & Events	+					

Key: + = cross mapping, ✔ = intra-mapping

Table 1 shows that the source domains of metaphorical sentences are usually concrete concepts. Human beings, animals, plants and objects all serve as the source domains of metaphorical mappings. Human beings and animals are the most important source domains. They can be mapped onto all the other things. Plants and objects can only be the prototypes for man, objects and abstracts. While the source domain only includes the concrete concepts, the target domain is more variable. It includes both the concrete concepts and the abstract ones. While the concrete may be metaphorized, the abstract usually has to be modeled on concrete things. The former often results in metaphors of substitution, and the latter usually results in metaphors of designation.

2.4 Generative Mechanisms of Metaphorical Sentences in Chinese

As shown in the previous section, English metaphorical sentences are generated through the mechanisms of personification, animalization, plantification, hypostatization and alienation. These mechanisms are not specific to English. They are also true in Chinese. Chinese metaphorical sentences are generated via the same mechanisms of personification, animalization, plantification, hypostatization and alienation.

2.4.1 Personification

Since people in all cultures develop the first and most striking understanding of themselves, they have much more knowledge of human beings than of other things. It is natural for Chinese people to understand other things in terms of humans and thus map human features, actions and behaviours onto other nonhuman things. When the nonhumans are expressed in human terms, a metaphorical sentence results.

2.4.1.1 Animals Personified

As in the English culture, Chinese people also find it easy and convenient to map human beings on their animal cousins. They project the knowledge of humans on their closest neighbours. Thus animals adopt human features, behaviours and actions. For example:

(58) 顽皮的海豚*掀翻了*他们的独木舟。

(59) 油蛉在这里*低唱*，蟋蟀在这里*弹琴*。

(60) 金蝉*操琴*蝴蝶*舞*，青蛙蝈蝈*打锣鼓*。

In the examples above, animals are modeled on human beings and expressed as such. Therefore, the animals can act and behave as people do. In (58), *the naughty dolphin* can *turn over* the canoe as if it had hands as human beings do. In (59), *the sand flies* can *sing* and *the crickets* can *play musical instruments*. In (60), *the golden cicada* can *play the musical instruments*, *butterflies* can *dance*, and *frogs* and *longhorn grasshoppers* can *beat drums*. All these animal Subjects do things that are usually done by human beings.

2.4.1.2 Plants Personified

In English, plants can take human beings as their prototypes, so can plants in Chinese. For example:

(61) 遍地谷子黄又黄，吊吊足有一尺长，*羞羞答答低着头*，怕人说他是高粱。

(62) 桃树、杏树、梨树，你不*让*我，我不*让*你，都开满了花赶趟儿。

(63) 牵牛花只*知道*有清晨，不*知道*有炎昼和黑夜。

(64) 那高大强壮油光发亮的橡皮树，*垂头丧气*，危在旦夕。

Here, plants are modeled on human beings. Since they are personified, they adopt human features and actions. Therefore, *the millet* in (61) *is shy* and so *lowers its head*. *The peach*, *almond* and *pear trees* in (62) do not *yield* to one another as if they had consciousness. *The morning glory* in (63) *knows* that there are mornings but it *does not know* that there are days and nights. In (64), *the balatas lower their heads* and *lose their spirits*.

2.4.1.3 Objects Personified

Inanimate objects in Chinese are often considered as persons as in English, so they share human motivations, characteristics, and activities. Here are some examples:

(65) 在山谷深处，丛林遮住的地方，两条年轻的小径胆怯地*接吻*。

(66) 刺骨的山风忽地*闯进来*，*打转身又出去*，*出出进进由着意窜*，一点也*不客气*。

(67) 血雨腥风里，毛竹青了又黄，黄了又青，不向残暴*低头*，不向敌人*弯腰*。

(68) 一捆捆的稿纸从屋角里的两只麻袋中*探头探脑地露出脸来*。

In each of these sentences, Chinese people are seeing something nonhuman as human. In (65), since *the two new paths* are personified, they can *kiss* each other shyly. Similarly in (66), *the piercing wind* is experienced as a person, so it can *rush in*, *turn round* and *go out once and again impolitely*. In (67), *the bamboos* are considered as humans and hence described as not *being willing to bend their heads* to the violence or *to bend their bodies* to the enemies. In (68), *the papers* are personified, so they can *pop their heads out* and *show their faces*.

2.4.1.4 Abstracts Personified

When abstracts are expressed in English, they have to be concretized first in the mind. Only after the mind admits that there is such a thing can it be referred to, talked about, qualified, quantified and modified. It is the same in Chinese. In the following sentences, abstracts are personified:

(69) 科技是*排头兵*。
(70) 医疗费用有望*走*“下坡路”。
(71) 理想主义*隐退*到社会主义的边缘。
(72) 这里叫教条主义*休息*，有些同志却叫它*起床*。

In all the examples above, the abstract concepts are considered as human beings, so *science* and *technology* can be *soldiers* at the head of a formation, *fees for medical service* can *walk* downward, *idealism* can *withdraw* and *live* in seclusion, and *dogmatism* can *take a rest* or *get up*.

2.4.1.5 Facts and Events Personified

As in English, facts and events can also be personified in Chinese. For example:

(73) 您的出席，*帮*了我们大忙。
(74) 这位大科学家对我们的评价，*给*了我们很大鼓舞。

In the two examples, facts and events are personified, so one can *help* and the other can *give* us encouragement.

It should be noted that such sentences, though somewhat westernized, are used more and more frequently in Chinese under the influence of foreign languages.

2.4.2 Animalization

Metaphorical sentences in English can be generated via animalization. Human beings, plants, objects and abstracts can all take animals as their prototypes and model themselves on animals. Chinese follows the same principle, and similar metaphorical sentences are found in everyday language.

2.4.2.1 Human Beings Animalized

In Chinese, human beings can be metaphorized as animals, so they can adopt animal features, actions and behaviours. Look at the following examples:

(75) 我和你，我们可以*飞*，*飞*到一个真真干净、快乐的地方。

(76) 我到了自家的房外，我的母亲早已迎着出来了，接着便*飞出*了八岁的侄女宏儿。

(77) 我从此要在新的开阔的天空中*翱翔*。

(78) 他*摇尾*乞怜了。

In the examples above, people are considered as animals and described as such. They can *fly* and *flutter* in (75), (76) and (77) when they are modeled on birds. In (78), a person is said to *wag his tail* as an animal, though he does not have one.

2.4.2.2 Plants Animalized

Plants can also be considered as animals and expressed as such in Chinese. Here are some examples:

(79) *飞*下来很多树叶。

(80) 各种兰花也*飞*到大树的顶上或中间。

(81) 墙上*爬*满了牵牛花。

Each of the examples above involves modeling plants on animals. *The leaves* or *the orchids* in (79) and (80) are modeled on birds, so they can *flutter* and *fly*. *The morning glories* in (81) are patterned on animals which can climb, such as monkeys.

2.4.2.3 Objects Animalized

Physical objects in Chinese often take animals as their prototypes and model themselves on animals. Look at the following examples:

(82) 风一刮，尘土全*飞*起来了。
(83) 小飞娥抬头看看他的脸，看见他的眼睛要*吃人*……
(84) 雨季刚刚过去，空气凝固咸腥，海寂寂寞寞*爬行*着。

In these examples, inanimate objects are experienced as animals. *The dust* in (82) is considered as birds and hence can *fly*. *His eyes* in (83) are regarded as fierce animals, so they can *eat people*. In (84) *the sea* is modeled on an animal that can crawl, such as snakes.

2.4.2.4 Abstracts Animalized

Abstract notions can be animalized in English, so can they in Chinese. For instance:

(85) 心中的歌儿*展翅*飞。
(86) 我的思想也在自由地飞*翔*。
(87) 一些目光蜂拥而来*蜇*他的脸。

In these examples, abstract notions are comprehended as animals. *Songs* in the heart in (85) and *my ideas* in (86) are experienced as birds, so that they can *spread their wings* and *fly*. In (87), *the looks of people* are considered as bees or wasps, so they can *sting*.

2.4.3 Plantification

As in English, plants conveniently help people understand other things in Chinese. In other words, plants serve as the source domains and are mapped on other things. The knowledge of plants is projected on things other than plants.

2.4.3.1 Human Beings Plantified

Though people know themselves very well on the basis of their own experiences, sometimes they find it convenient to conceive and describe themselves in terms of plants. For instance:

(88) 知识青年已经在农场*扎了根*。

(89) 好林子，一架山森森的引眼。不想再走，情愿将自己*栽*在这里，也绿绿的活个痛快。

(90) 青年时代结交的战斗伙伴，相继*凋谢*，实在使人感怆不已。

In the examples above, human beings are understood as plants and therefore are expressed as plants. They can *be rooted* on the farm in (88), *be planted* in (89) as if they were grass or trees. They can *shrivel* in (90) as if they were flowers or grass.

2.4.3.2 Abstracts Plantified

In Chinese, abstract notions can be plantified and understood as plants. For example:

(91) 她的美的确那样浓烈而不易*凋谢*。

(92) 中国的新文学运动，方在*萌芽*……

(93) 他心里*萌发*出一个崭新的念头。

(94) 难道我们就*根除*不了蝗害了吗？

Each of the examples above involves mapping the concept of plants on the abstract concepts. In (91), *her beauty* is experienced as flowers that do not easily *wither*. *The movement of the new-vernacular literature in China* in (92) is considered as seeds, so is *a new idea* in (93). In (94), *the plague of locusts* is understood as plants in general, so they might *be uprooted*.

2.4.4 Hypostatization

Hypostatization is also a generative mechanism of Chinese metaphorical sentences. Inanimate objects are usually mapped onto animate things and abstracts.

2.4.4.1 Human Beings and Animals Hypostatized

Animate things may transfer toward the source domain of the inanimate substance. For example:

(95) 他简直累*垮*了。
(96) 我们场的两个技术人员可以*流动*。
(97) 福建一男子将买来的男孩“*邮寄*回乡”。
(98) 一只蝴蝶正*停泊*在她那头发流成的小溪里。

In the examples above, animate things are understood as inanimate objects. In (95), (96) and (97), human beings are experienced as physical objects while in (98), an animal is considered as a tangible substance. Therefore, a person in (95) can *collapse* as a solid object. In (96), the two technicians can *flow* as if they were liquids. *The boy* in (97) is thought of as a parcel and thus can *be mailed*. *A butterfly* in (98) is metaphorized as a ship or a boat so that it can *anchor* in the stream of her hair.

2.4.4.2 Abstracts Hypostatized

As in English, abstracts are usually hypostatized. They are

experienced as physical substances. They adopt the features and behaviours of the inanimate objects. For instance:

(99) 牛儿悠闲地*反刍*着*岁*月。

(100) 我将*深味*这非人间的浓黑的悲凉……

(101) 我*给*他个不辞而别。

(102) 他是把部队的老传统*扔掉*了，把解放区人民的心意*扔掉*了，把他自己的荣誉*扔掉*了。

In these cases, abstract notions are considered as inanimate objects. In (99) and (100), *the years* and *the strong inhuman sorrow* are understood as food, so they can *be chewed* and *tasted*. In (101), *the action of leaving without saying goodbye* is regarded as an inanimate substance and hence it can *be given* to others. What are hypostatized in (102) are the abstract concepts of *the old tradition of the army*, *the regards of the masses* in the liberated areas and *the honour of himself*, so they can all *be thrown away*.

2.4.5 Alienation

As in English, alienation in Chinese involves mapping one kind of concrete thing onto another. One physical object can be understood as another. One kind of person can be considered as another. For example:

(103) 人民教师是培养祖国后代的*园丁*。

(104) 作家、记者和编辑都是语言的*工程师*。

(105) 走吧，冰上的月光，已从河床上*溢出*。

(106) 一乡一镇，动辄数百万的债务，这钱，都*流*到哪里去了？

(107) 山，*刺破*青天锷未残。

(108) 只有清晨才具有的鲜红的阳光，正在那个天空里*飘扬*。

In (103) and (104), one kind of person is understood as another and expressed as another. *Teachers* in (103) are described as *gardeners,* and *writers*, *reporters* and *editors* in (104) are said to be *engineers*. In all the other four sentences, one physical object is experienced as another. *The moonbeams* in (105) and *money* in (106) are considered as liquids such as water, so they can *flow* or *overflow*. In (107), *the mountain* is regarded as a knife or a dagger so that it can *stab* into the sky. In (108), *the sunshine* is experienced as a flag that flies high in the sky.

2.4.6 Summary

In this section, the generative mechanisms of metaphorical sentences in Chinese are brought into discussion. They are personification, animalization, plantification, hypostatization and alienation. The generative mechanisms of metaphorical sentences in Chinese can be summarized in Table 2:

Table 2 Generative Mechanisms of Metaphorical Sentences in Chinese

Source / Target	Human Beings	Animals	Plants	Objects	Abstracts	Facts & Events
Human Beings	✔	+	+	+		
Animals	+			+		
Plants	+	+				
Objects	+	+		✔		
Abstracts	+	+	+	+		
Facts & Events	+					

Key: + = cross mapping, ✔ = intra-mapping

Table 2 shows that the source domains of metaphorical sentences in Chinese are usually concrete concepts. Human beings, animals, plants and objects all serve as source domains of metaphorical mappings. Human beings and animals are the most important source domains. They can be mapped onto all the other things. Plants can only be the prototypes for man and abstracts, and objects can serve as the source domain of human beings, animals, abstracts and other objects. While the source domain only consists of the concrete concepts, the target domain is wider. It includes both concrete and abstract concepts. While the concrete may be metaphorized, the abstract usually has to be modeled on concrete things. The former often results in substitutional metaphors, and the latter usually results in designatory metaphors.

2.5 Summary and Discussion

This chapter has made a rather detailed study of the generative mechanisms of metaphorical sentences in English and Chinese. It is shown that some sentences in both English and Chinese are generated through metaphorization. In other words, metaphorization is the generative mechanism of some sentences. Sentences generated via metaphorization are metaphorical sentences. These metaphorical sentences are made by mapping one thing or one kind of thing onto another. As for the specific mechanisms, English and Chinese share the same metaphorized processes of personification, animalization, plantification, hypostatization and alienation.

In order to show more clearly the contrast between English and

Chinese metaphorical sentences, their generative mechanisms are summarized in Table 3:

Table 3 Generative Mechanisms of Metaphorical Sentences in English and Chinese

Source / Target	Human Beings		Animals		Plants		Objects		Abstracts		Facts & Events	
	E.	C.	E.	C.	E.	C.	E.	C.	E.	C.	E.	C.
Human Beings	✔	✔	+	+	+	+	+	+				
Animals	+	+						+				
Plants	+	+	+	+								
Objects	+	+	+	+	+		✔	✔				
Abstracts	+	+	+	+	+	+	+	+				
Facts & Events	+	+										

Key: E. = English, C. = Chinese, + = cross mapping, ✔ = intra-mapping

Table 3 shows that personification and animalization are the most important generative mechanisms for both the two languages. This is because human beings and animals are the most active concrete things. They provide the most striking features and the earliest cognitive patterns in the human mind. All other things can be understood in terms of human beings and animals. Even nonentities can be experienced as human.

Besides human beings and animals, plants and objects also function as prototypes for cross-domain mappings in the two languages. While plants can be mapped on human beings, objects and abstracts in English, they can only be projected on human beings and abstracts in Chinese. In conceptualizing things in terms of objects, English can only model human beings and abstracts on physical substance, but Chinese can model human beings, animals and abstracts on concrete objects. As for alienation, English and Chinese follow the same principle of mapping one kind of concrete thing onto another, specifically, from one kind of person to another and from one kind of object to another.

However, two points must be kept in mind. One is that none of the generative mechanisms is a single unified general process (Lakoff & Johnson, 1980: 33). For example, each personification may differ in terms of the aspects of people that are picked out. Consider these examples from Lakoff & Johnson:

Inflation has attacked the foundation of our country.
Inflation has pinned us to the wall.
Our biggest enemy right now is inflation.
The dollar has been destroyed by inflation.
Inflation has robbed me of my savings.
Inflation has outwitted the best economic minds in the country.
Inflation has given birth to a money-minded generation.

Here *inflation* is personified, but the metaphor is not merely INFLATION IS A PERSON. It is much more specific, for instance, INFLATION IS AN ADVERSARY. It not only gives us a very specific way of thinking about inflation but also a way of acting on it. We think of inflation as an adversary that can attack us, hurt us, steal from us, even destroy us. The INFLATION IS AN ADVERSARY metaphor therefore gives rise to and justifies political and economic actions on the part of our government: declaring war on inflation, setting targets, calling for sacrifices, installing a new chain of command, etc.

The point here is that personification is a general category that covers a very wide range of metaphors, each picking out different aspects of a person or ways of looking at a person. What they all have in common is that they are extensions of "ontological metaphors" (Lakoff & Johnson, 1980: 34) and that they allow us to make sense of phenomena in the world in human terms—terms that we can understand on the basis of our own motivation, goals, actions, and characteristics. Viewing something as abstract as inflation in human terms has an explanatory power of the only sort that makes sense to most people. When we are suffering substantial economic losses due to complex economic and political factors that no one really understands, the INFLATION IS AN ADVERSARY metaphor at least gives us a coherent account of why we're suffering these losses.

Similar with personification, animalization is not a single unified general process. Each animalization differs in terms of the aspects of animals that are picked out. Sometimes non-animals are understood as a bird, sometimes as a snake, sometimes as a hen, a dog, a bee, etc. Therefore, animalization is a general category that covers a wide range of metaphors, each highlighting different aspects of animals or ways of looking at animals. What they all have in common is that they enable us to comprehend phenomena in the world in animal terms, terms we know on the basis of our experiences with animals.

Plantification and hypostatization are not single unified general processes, either. The prototypes for plant metaphors may be grass, flowers or trees or even specific kinds of grass, flower or tree. The source domain of hypostatization is much wider. As the examples in 2.3.4 and 2.4.4 indicate, the objects can be a plough, water, products, machines, a parcel, a ship, food, etc.

The second point is that there is no clearcut distinction between the generative mechanisms of metaphorical sentences though we classify them into different kinds for convenience of discussion. Sometimes it is not so easy to distinguish one mechanism from another. First of all, it is difficult to distinguish personification from animalization, since human beings and their animal cousins share many similarities. Some human action and behaviour and animal action and behaviour are the same. They are both the earliest cognitive patterns in man's mind. For example:

(109) The cash machine *ate* my card.

Obviously the machine here is modeled on an animate thing. But it is hard to say whether the thing modeled on is a human or an animal. That is why some researchers do not distinguish personification from animalization, but just use the term "animatization" (Yang Lili, 1997: 75) to include both. However, the general term is not so proper and inclusive because animate things also include plants.

Sometimes it is also difficult to distinguish among personification, animalization and plantification because human beings, animals and plants are the three general classes of animate things. They naturally have some resemblances in their features, behaviour and action. Look at the following sentences:

(110) The village *is growing* into a town.

(111) 两次竞赛获胜后，同学们中间渐渐*生长*了骄傲自满情绪。

The predicate verb *grow* means to increase in number or in size. It is usually used to describe the natural development of animate things, that is, humans, animals or plants. Therefore, it requires an animate Subject. But the Subjects of the two sentences here are not animate. One is a physical object, and the other is an abstract. They are both modeled on an animate thing, whatever it is.

What is important here is that animate behaviours and actions are the most important deposits of the source domains for generating metaphorical expressions. Human beings, animals and plants can all be prototypes for metaphorical mappings. If cross mappings are involved, there emerges a metaphorical sentence, although sometimes it is not easy to tell exactly what the source domain is.

Chapter Three

Representation of Subject-verb Transitivity Systems of Metaphorical Sentences in English and Chinese

Chapter Two deals with the generative mechanisms of metaphorical sentences in English and Chinese. This chapter and the next one will discuss the representation of metaphorical sentences in the two languages. In order to make a detailed study of this question, the conventional ways of expressing things and their relationship should be discussed. In this respect, we resort to Halliday's concept of transitivity systems, or verb processes. Without the knowledge of the inherent semantic features and grammatical features of each type of process, it is impossible to know whether a process is used congruently or metaphorically.

As mentioned in 1.4.2, when man gets to know the world, he does it not merely by impressing the names of the separate things on his mind, but by realizing an individual thing's features, behaviour, action and its relation with other things. All these can be typically expressed in a transitivity system of verb processes. The features, for example, can be represented by a relational process, the behaviour by a behavioural process, and the happening by a material process or an abstract entity process. Therefore, when one thing is modeled on another, it also adopts the features, the behaviour or the action of the other, as has been discussed in Chapter Two. In other words, one process may be modeled on and express the meaning of other processes by means of metaphorization. The incongruence of process realization indicates that a metaphorical sentence is brought into being. The incongruent realization of processes can be represented by Subject-verb transitivity systems, verb-Object transitivity systems, and Subject-verb-Object/Complement transitivity systems. Representation of Subject-verb transitivity systems in metaphorical sentences will be the topic of this chapter. The next chapter will tackle the representation of verb-Object and Subject-verb-Object/ Complement transitivity systems in metaphorical sentences.

3.1 Transitivity Systems

The theory of transitivity is an important part of Halliday's systemic functional grammar. It is also one of Halliday's most remarkable contributions to the study of grammar. However, the following discussion of the process types is not exactly in accordance with Halliday. What it provides is a logical classification of process types according to the general classes of things and their actions.

According to Halliday (1994: 106), a fundamental property of language is that it "enables human beings to build a mental picture of reality, to make sense of their experience of what goes on around them and inside them". "All these goings-on are sorted out in the grammar of the clause", so "the clause is ... a mode of reflection, of imposing orders on the endless variation and the flow of events". "The grammatical system by which this is achieved is TRANSITIVITY. The transitivity system construes the world of experience into a manageable set of PROCESS TYPES."

The term transitivity will probably be familiar as a way of distinguishing between verbs according to whether they have an Object or not. Here, however, it is being used in a much broader sense. As shown above, it refers to a system for describing the whole clause, rather than just the verb and its Object. However, it does share with the traditional use a focus on the verbal group, since it is the type of process that determines what participants are involved and how they are labeled.

A process consists, in principle, of three components: the process proper, the participants in the process, and the circumstances associated with the process. This tripartite interpretation of processes is in accordance with Marxist philosophy, which maintains that the world is composed of entities that are in constant motion in particular circumstances. It also agrees with what lies behind the grammatical distinction of word classes into verbs, nouns and the rest. The process is typically expressed—or realized—by a verbal group in the clause, and is the central component of the message. The participants are normally realized by nominal groups while circumstances are typically realized by adverbial groups or prepositional phrases. Normally every process includes at least one participant, represented either by the Subject or by the Object; but circumstances are often optional, reflecting the background function of time, place, manner, cause, result, etc., in the clause. Therefore, the following discussion of the process types leaves out the circumstantial elements.

The concepts of process, participant and circumstance are semantic categories which explain in the most general way how phenomena of the real world are represented as linguistic structures. When particular types of processes are interpreted, more specific categories are adopted. Nevertheless, they all derive from and can be related to these three general categories.

According to Halliday, transitivity systems include six processes: material, mental, relational, behavioural, verbal and existential. However, his classification seems to be too general, so the boundaries between the process types appear to be too vague to be manageable. One example is the existential process. In Halliday's opinion, besides the typically used verb *be*, other verbs also occur in the process. "One group is a small set of closely related verbs meaning 'exist' or 'happen': *exist, remain, arise; occur, come about, happen, take place*. The other group embody some circumstantial feature; e.g. of time (*follow, ensue*), place (*sit, stand, lie, hang, rise, stretch, emerge, grow*). But a considerable number of other verbs can also be used in a range of abstract existential clauses; e.g. *erupt, flourish, prevail.*" (Halliday, 1994: 142) (original, the author) However, these verb processes are not considered as existential in this book. They belong to other processes. Therefore, this book will offer a different classification of the process types according to the general categories of things and their actions. Altogether there are eight process types in the transitivity systems: material processes, abstract entity processes, sensuous processes, behavioural processes, mental processes, verbal processes, relational processes and existential processes. Moreover, many process types are understood differently from Halliday's in this book.

In the following sections, we shall explore the different types of processes and the particular kinds of participant roles that are systematically associated with each process. Though Halliday just talks about the transitivity systems in English, he hints that the interpretation of processes in terms of verbs, nouns, and the rest is "a pattern that in some form or other is probably universal among human languages" (Halliday, 1994: 108). Therefore, it is assumed that the following discussion of the process types is applicable to both English and Chinese.

3.1.1 Material Processes

Material processes in this book are very different from those of Halliday's. They are the processes of happenings of inanimate objects. In other words, material processes refer to physical processes. They express the notion that something happens to some object or that some object does something—which may be done "to" some other object. Any verb implying the physical action of an inanimate object belongs to this type of process. The doer of this type of action is called the Actor: any material process has an Actor, even though the Actor may not actually be mentioned in the clause. In some cases, the action may be represented as affecting or being done to a second participant. This participant is called the Goal, since the action is, in a sense, directed at this participant. Therefore, material processes are usually encoded in the sentence patterns of SV and SVO. For example:

(1) The glass broke.
(2) The car slithered off the road.
(3) The fire had destroyed everything.

The three sentences above are all in the material processes. They are used to express the happenings of the inanimate objects. (1) and (2) are expressed in SV pattern and (3) in SVO pattern.

3.1.2 Abstract Entity Processes

Abstract entity processes are the processes of the happenings of abstract entities. The so-called abstract entities refer to physical or social phenomena which are not real physical entities, but are treated as such in human mind such as safety, worry, agreement, etc. The doer of this type of action is labeled the Experiencer. It is usually the only participant of the process. Therefore, abstract entity processes are normally realized by SV pattern. For example:

(4) When did the accident happen?
(5) A robbery took place.
(6) His death occurred the following year.

The three sentences above are all in the abstract entity processes. They are all used to express the happenings of abstract entities, and realized in SV pattern.

3.1.3 Sensuous Processes

Sensuous processes in this research include the minor processes of affection and perception in Halliday's mental processes. They are the processes of sensing of animate things, including plants and animals, especially human beings.

Halliday (1994: 106) groups together clauses of feeling, thinking and perceiving under the general heading of mental processes, because all the three processes express "the inner experience", or "what we experience as going on inside ourselves, in the world of consciousness and imagination".

Though Halliday is right in claiming that all the three minor processes of perception, affection and cognition are used to express the inner experience, they are intuitively different. The processes of perception and affection share more similarities than they do with the process of cognition. Therefore, they are labeled sensuous processes in this book.

"In deciding what types of process to recognize, we resort to a combination of common sense and grammar: common sense to distinguish the different kinds of 'goings-on' that we can identify, and grammar to confirm that these intuitive differences are reflected in language and thus to justify the decision to set up a separate category. We need to set up categories that are detailed enough to make us feel that we have captured something important about meaning, but broad enough to be manageable as the basis for general claims about the grammar of English [and other languages]." (Thompson, 1996: 79)

Intuitively, perception is the first step by which man gets to know the world via sensory organs, which are conveniently classified into five types: visual, auditory, olfactory, gustatory and tactile. Visual perception is the most important one, with the tactile, the auditory, the olfactory and the gustatory following in succession. "The quality of our perceptual experience depends ... on the stimuli that impinge on our sense organs and the signals directly induced by these stimuli." (Langacker, 1987: 101)

Similarly, affection also depends on the outer stimuli that attract our sensory organs. Thompson even uses the word "reaction" (Thompson, 1996: 85) to define it. All affections seem to be the result of outer input. Moreover, most emotions bring about physiological effects on the person who has the emotions. These physiological and sometimes physical effects are most of the time visible and sensible to the sense organs of others. Therefore, perception and affection are closely connected.

On the contrary, "though sensory stimulation lays the foundation and provides the raw material for the construction of our conceptual world, often we do not attend to it ..." (Langacker, 1987: 112). So conception is different from affection and perception.

Grammatically, while perception and affection processes can have actions as "the objects of consciousness" (Halliday, 1994: 115), it seems that the cognition processes cannot. For example:

Perception:

(7) I heard the water lapping on the crag.
(8) I saw the boats turning.

Affection:

(9) I don't like your talking to me like that.
(10) Most students enjoy asking questions in English.

Another reason to distinguish the three processes into two is theory-oriented. Theoretically, the distinction can help us understand better how language works, as will be shown throughout the following two chapters. While sensuous processes can serve as the source domains of metaphorical mappings, mental processes usually cannot.

In the sensuous processes, the animate participant is the Senser, and the other participant which is sensed is the Phenomenon. Sensuous processes all involve two participants and are usually incorporated into SVO pattern. For example:

(11) Jane saw the stars.
(12) She could hear his voice.
(13) Mary liked that present.
(14) The gift pleased Mary.
(15) The cat doesn't like the milk.

All these sentences are in the sensuous processes. They are encoded to express the sensing of animate entities. The Sensers of (11), (12), (13) and (14) are human beings, and that of (15) is an animal. They are all expressed in SVO pattern.

However, this does not mean that both participants must always be present in the clause. Either can be absent, but "it is particularly the Phenomenon that may be omitted: omission of the Senser tends to occur in more restricted context" (Thompson, 1996: 86). For instance:

(16) Jill can't see.
(17) He only does it to annoy.

In (16), the Phenomenon is omitted. What Jill can't see is not expressed. It may be a blackboard, a screen, or even anything if, for example, she loses her eyesight. In (17), however, the Senser is absent. The implicit Senser is simply "people".

3.1.4 Behavioural Processes

Behavioural processes are the processes of behaviours and

doings of animate beings. They express the meaning that some animate being does something. They may involve both physical doings such as running, throwing, scratching, cooking, sitting down, coughing, smiling etc., and abstract doings such as resigning, dissolving, permitting. The doer of this type of action is called the Behaver: any behavioural process has a Behaver, even though the Behaver may not actually be mentioned in the clause. In many cases, the behaviour may be represented as affecting or being done to a second participant. This participant is called the Patient, which is often represented by the direct Object. Another possible participant is the Recipient, which is usually represented by the indirect Object. Therefore, behavioural processes are usually encoded in the sentence patterns of SV, SVO and SVOO. For example:

(18) We all laughed.
(19) The lion sprang.
(20) She sang a song.
(21) Edward was sawing the wood.
(22) The lion caught the tourist.
(23) The mayor dissolved the committee.
(24) He painted John a picture.

In the sentences above, the Behavers represented by the Subject in (18), (20), (21), (23) and (24) are all human beings, and those of (19) and (22) are animals. All the verbal groups express physical or abstract doings of animate things. Therefore, the sentences are all in the behavioural processes. (18) and (19) are in SV pattern, (20), (21), (22) and (23) in SVO pattern and (24) in SVOO pattern.

3.1.5 Mental Processes

Mental processes in this book indicate the processes of cognition. They are processes of thinking, believing and conceiving, etc., of human beings. They always involve two participants. One is the human participant who thinks, believes and conceives. The other is the set of things that are thought about, believed and conceived. The human participant is labeled the Thinker and the set of things Thought. Mental processes are usually encoded in SVO pattern. For example:

(25) You can imagine his reaction.
(26) No one believed his story.
(27) He conceived a bold plan for escape.

Though mental processes always involve two participants, this is not to say that the clause invariably has two participants expressed. Either participant may be omitted. For instance:

(28) Do you think in English when you speak English?
(29) The situation was even worse than was supposed.

In (28), the Thought is absent. The clause does not make explicit what the particular Thought is. In (29), however, the Thinker is absent. The implied Thinker is simply "people".

3.1.6 Verbal Processes

Verbal processes are the processes of sayings of human beings. Different from Halliday's interpretation of saying in a rather broad sense to cover any kind of symbolic exchange of meaning, saying is defined in this work in a rather narrow sense. It only covers the action of sayings of human beings. The verbs used in the verbal processes are *speak*, *tell*, *say* and those that can be replaced by *speak*, *tell* or *say* with some modification. The human participant involved is the Sayer. Another participant that may be involved, and that is also typically human, is the Receiver: the participant to whom the saying is addressed. In certain cases, the verbal processes may be directed at rather than addressed to another participant. The participant is called the Target. The message itself is called the Verbiage. Structurally, verbal processes are realized in the sentence patterns of SVO and SVOO. For example:

(30) He can speak several languages.
(31) I told him my name.
(32) John said he was hungry.
(33) He claimed to be the right heir.

All the sentences above are in the verbal processes since they express the saying actions of human beings. (30), (32) and (33) are in SVO pattern, and (31) is in SVOO pattern.

3.1.7 Relational Processes

Relational processes are "those of being" (Halliday, 1994: 119) of two physical entities or of one physical entity and its feature or property. In relational clauses, there are two parts to the "being": something is being said to "be" something else. In other words, a relation is being set up "to relate one fragment of experience to another: this is the same as that, this is a kind of the other" (Halliday, 1994: 107).

Relational processes fall into two distinct modes: attributive and identifying. Each of these operates with three main types: intensive, circumstantial and possessive. In the attributive mode, an entity has some quality ascribed or attributed to it. Structurally, we label this quality as the Attribute, and the entity to which it is ascribed is the Carrier. In the identifying mode, some thing has an identity assigned to it. What is meant is that one entity is being used to identify another. What is to be identified is labeled as the Identified, and what serves as the identity as the Identifier. The most important difference between the attributive mode and the identifying mode is that the identifying modes are reversible. Relational processes usually involve two participants and are normally incorporated in the sentence patterns of SVC and SVO. For example:

Attributive processes:

(34) Sarah is wise.

(35) The village is on the mountain.

(36) Peter has a piano.

Identifying processes:

(37) Tom is the leader. / The leader is Tom.

(38) Beijing is the capital of China. / The capital of China is Beijing.

(39) The piano is Peter's. / Peter's is the piano.

All these examples express the relation between two physical entities except (34), which expresses the relation between a physical entity and its attribute. They are all realized in SVC pattern except (36), which is realized in SVO pattern.

One point to be noticed is that some relational processes in Chinese do not contain a verb. That means the verb process itself is covert. For instance:

(40) 她(V)很漂亮。

(41) 这房子(V)真大。

3.1.8 Existential Processes

The final process type is the existential process, which expresses the existence of a physical entity. There is only one participant in such clauses: the Existent. Existential processes are normally recognizable in English because the Subject is "there", which "has no representational function" (Halliday, 1994: 142) and the verb is usually *be* or different forms of *be*. Other details concerning the Existent can be given in the circumstantial elements. An existential process in Chinese usually has three components: a location represented by a Subject, the process proper represented by a verb and the Existent represented by an Object. The predicate verb is *有*, which means existing rather than owning or possessing. Therefore, both English and Chinese existential processes are realized in SVO sentence pattern. For example:

(42) There is a book on the table.

(43) There was a picture on the wall.

(44) 桌子上有一本书。

(45) 墙上有一幅画。

3.1.9 Summary

This section has given a brief description of the transitivity systems or process types and the participant roles associated with each. The eight important process types are no doubt very general, so that they embrace all the possible occurrences in the outside world as well as man's inner world. Each type has its semantic and grammatical features. Table 4 gives a summary of the types of processes, together with their general category meaning, the principal participant functions and the commonly used sentence patterns that are associated with each.

Table 4 Overview of Transitivity Systems

Process type	Category meaning	Features of the participants	Sentence patterns
Material	happening	1. Inani. Obj. Actor ∧ verb 2. Inani. Obj. Actor ∧ verb ^ Obj. Goal	SV SVO
Abstract Entity	happening	1. Abs. Ent. Experiencer ∧ verb	SV
Sensuous	sensing	1. Ani. esp. Hum. Senser ∧ Ani. verb ∧ Phe. 2. Phe. ∧ Ani. verb ∧ Ani. esp. Hum. Senser	SVO SV
Behavioural	behaving doing	1. Ani. esp. Hum. Behaver ∧ Ani. verb 2. Ani. esp. Hum. Behaver ∧Ani. verb ∧ Patient 3. Ani. esp. Hum. Behaver ∧ Ani. verb ∧ Recipient ∧ Patient	SV SVO SVOO
Mental	thinking	1. Hum. Thinker ∧ Ani. verb ∧ Thought	SVO SV
Verbal	saying	1. Hum. Sayer ∧ Ani. verb ∧ Target 2. Hum. Sayer ∧ Ani. verb ∧ Verbiage 3. Hum. Sayer ∧ Ani. verb ∧ Hum. Receiver ∧ Verbiage	SVO SVOO
Relational Attributive Identifying	being attribute identity	1. Obj. Carrier ∧ Attribute 2. Obj. Identified ∧ Identifier	SVC SVO
Existential	existing	1. Obj. Existent	SVO

Key: Inani. = inanimate, Obj. = object, Abs. Ent. = abstract entity, Ani. = animate, Hum. = human, Phe. = Phenomenon

In designing the table, the author still relies on the following terms: entity, object, animate, inanimate, plant, animal and human since they are assumed to be the most essential categories in the outside world and in human experience that have obtained established patterns in language. The relations can be expressed as: entity > object > inanimate / animate > plant / animal > human, with the sign ">" signifying "bigger than" or "including" and the sign "/" signifying "parallel to". If there are no modifiers before a semantic category, it means that the semantic category includes any entity, either physical or abstract. However, there are usually modifiers before the semantic categories. So, for example, "Obj. Existent" means that Existent is typically used for expressing the existence of objects, including both the inanimate objects and the animate objects, namely, plants, animals and human beings.

Table 4 shows the stereotype of each process. While some processes only have one stereotype, some processes may have two or three stereotypes, according to the meaning of the verb processes and the participants involved. Correspondingly, the processes can be encoded differently in SV, SVO, SVC or SVOO sentence patterns. Most of the participants in the eight processes are either physical or abstract entities. Actually, all participants except for the Attribute in the relational process, must be a physical or abstract entity since these processes are established to express what man experiences about himself and the outside world.

However, several points must be explained. The first point is that the stereotyped forms described in Table 4 are not designed exactly after earlier researchers. First, the classification of the process types is different. While Halliday only talks about six process types in language, there are eight in this book. The second difference lies in the relative status of the process types. According to Halliday, material, mental and relational processes are major processes, but behavioural, verbal and existential processes are minor processes. However, the author thinks that all the process types have equal status since they are used to represent different activities of different entities. Moreover, the semantic features of the process types are not the same. The Sayer in the verbal process, for example, is not necessarily a human being according to Halliday. But in this book it is restricted to a human in the hope that this restriction as well as the others will better illustrate the objective nature of language.

The second point to be noted is that the terms of the semantic categories are mainly borrowed from systemic functional grammar, especially from that of Halliday though they may not have the same meaning. Other necessary terms are either of my own coinage or from the adjacent fields of language study. All the terms are given an adequate definition or explanation. Take the term "Thinker" for example. It is used to indicate the human participant of the mental process. It means the person who thinks, believes or conceives.

The third point is that the boundaries of some process types are not clearcut. Many verbs can be used in different processes. Consider *protest* in the two examples *They protested strongly against such barbarous aggression* and *The seller protests that the price is depriving him of all profit*. It is used as a behavioural process in the former sentence but a verbal process in the latter.

The fourth point to be noted is that, for lack of time, this work cannot make a comprehensive study of all the verbs in English or Chinese, not to say the verbs in other languages. It is impossible to list all the verbs to be used in each process. The examples provided before and after are just the most typical ones. Some verbs are evaded in this book because the author could not feel quite sure about their nature.

Finally, several grammatical terms should be defined since they are often used in this book. They are discussed in pairs. The first pair are the animate verb and the inanimate verb. Animate verbs are verbs that require nouns representing animate things as their Subjects and inanimate verbs are verbs that require nouns representing inanimate things as their Subjects. The second pair are the animate Subject and the inanimate Subject. While the animate Subject is the Subject that is represented by a noun implying an animate thing, the inanimate Subject is the Subject that is represented by a noun implying an inanimate thing. The last pair are the animate sentence and the inanimate sentence. An animate sentence is a sentence that has an animate Subject, and an inanimate sentence is a sentence that has an inanimate Subject. On the basis of these definitions, other terms such as human Subject, animal Subject are easy to understand.

3.2 Representation of Subject-verb Transitivity Systems of Metaphorical Sentences in English

The preceding section has described the eight process types and their semantic and grammatical features. In other words, the stereotypes of the process types have been delineated. Each process type is used to represent a particular experience and involves particular participants. Grammatically, each clause is realized in certain kinds of structures and each participant is realized in certain grammatical units. However, language does not work in this easy way since the human mind reflects reality both passively and actively. Either the passive limitations or the active participation of the human mind in the reflection of reality will lead to incongruent realizations of the process types. If one process is used otherwise to express the meaning of another process, it is a metaphorical expression. Similarly, if one verb process does not have its normal realization of the participant roles, it also leads to an incongruent expression. Therefore, metaphorical sentences can be represented by mapping one process type onto another or one kind of participant onto another. The two kinds of mappings are usually related: the cross-process mappings often involve cross-participant mappings, and the inter-participant mappings also involve inter-process mappings.

Usually one process is used metaphorically instead of another on the basis of imaginary resemblance. For example, the sensuous processes are normally used to express sensing activities of animate things. If something other than animate beings is conceptualized imaginatively as an animate being, it can also sense. Therefore, sensuous processes can be encoded metaphorically to describe nonsensing of inanimate beings. Look at the following example:

(46) (a) Mary saw Tom in the city.
(b) <u>Beijing</u> first *saw* the rising of the five star red flag in Tian An Men Square.
(c) The first five star red flag rose in Tian An Men Square.

In this example, (a) is the stereotype expression of a sensuous process, and (b) is a metaphorical one, which consists of a sensuous verbal group *saw* but not an animate Senser. The metaphorical Senser is a location, i.e., Beijing, which is imagined as an animate being, especially a human, so it can *see* something happen. Therefore, (b) is generated via personification, one kind of metaphorical mechanism. Structurally, (b) is modeled on (a). The modeled process of (a) is the prototype, and the modeling process contained in the metaphorical sentence of (b) is the model. The prototype and the model are encoded in one and the same sentence pattern. The relationship between (a) and (b) is an embryological one. If there is a model, there must be a prototype. Semantically, (b) expresses the meaning of a material process of (c). The relationship between (b) and (c) is a synonymous one, i.e., a logical one.

In metaphorical mappings of the processes, the source domains or the prototype processes are normally those of the concrete and physical entities and the target domains or the model processes are typically those of the abstract and nonphysical entities. This is because the processes of the concrete and physical entities are usually more vivid, more dynamic and more remarkable to the human mind, so they are easily sensed and conceptualized. Actually many happenings of abstract entities are only expressed metaphorically in other processes without the congruent forms. They are the metaphors of designation. Consider the following examples about time:

(47) As I walked home, <u>the dawn</u> *was* just *breaking*.

(48) <u>Dusk</u> *was falling* as we left the place.

(49) The bitter <u>winter</u> *was coming*.

(50) <u>The day</u> *dragged by*.

(51) <u>National day</u> *drew* near.

(52) <u>Pleasant hours</u> *fly* fast.

(53) <u>Spring</u> *has gone* and summer is here.

(54) The ten days *passed* rapidly.

(55) The year *is progressing*.

All the examples above express the motion of time metaphorically. While (47) and (48) are in material processes, all the other sentences are in behavioural processes. In other words, material processes and behavioural processes are mapped on abstract entity processes and used metaphorically to realize their meaning. Note that the prototype sentences and the synonymous sentences are not given in these examples.

Besides the motion of time, other abstract entity processes are often modeled on and realized in other processes, too. For example:

(56) The temperature suddenly *dropped* to zero.

(57) Last year the retail price *fell* 20 percent.

(58) His spirits *fell* at the sad news.

(59) A great part of our health expenditure *goes* to the countryside.

(60) His temperature *jumped* sharply.

In these examples, the happenings of the abstract entities of temperature, price, spirits and expenditure are all expressed in other processes. While (56), (57) and (58) are in the material processes, (59) and (60) are in the behavioural processes. In order to save space, the prototype sentences and the synonymous sentences are not given in these examples, either.

Since the incongruent expressions above are designatory metaphors, it is often difficult to provide the synonymous expressions in the congruent forms. Therefore, the author, in the following discussion, sometimes simply leaves out the congruent forms of the abstract entity processes. For the other processes, though the congruent expressions are given, they are sometimes not congruent to reality but more congruent than the metaphorical ones. Moreover, some (more) congruent forms are not natural, so they are not commonly used.

However, though metaphorical mappings are often from the concrete to the abstract, this does not mean that the processes of the concrete and physical entities always serve as the prototypes for metaphorical transferences. While many processes of concrete and physical entities may function as both source domains and target domains, some processes seldom perform the function of the source domain. The cross mappings between processes of concrete and physical entities can be illustrated by example (46), which involves the transference from a sensuous process of an animate being to a material process of an inanimate object though the animate being and the inanimate object are both concrete and physical. The process that seldom serves as the prototype for cross mappings is the mental process, which is often modeled on other processes because the thinking process is so subtle and abstract that even man himself sometimes does not know how it proceeds.

Theoretically speaking, cross mappings may take place between any two different processes and intra-process mappings may take place within any type of process. Therefore, theoretically, metaphorical mappings total 64 ($8 \times 8 = 64$). Actually, there are not so many in a particular language.

English metaphorical sentences of Subject-verb transitivity systems can be represented in six processes, excepting the abstract entity process and the existential process. Actually, the abstract entity process can never serve as the source domain of other processes because metaphorical mappings are usually from the more concrete to the more abstract. The existential process cannot serve as the source domain of other processes in the Subject-verb transitivity systems in that the Subject in the existential process has "no representational function" (Halliday, 1994: 142). However, it may be the prototype for other processes in the Subject-verb-Object transitivity systems, as will be discussed in 4.3.6.

The six processes will be discussed one by one.

3.2.1 Material Processes

Since material processes express the happenings of inanimate objects, they appeal to visual sensation and spatial, kinetic perception. So, for the sake of vividness, they are usually preferred to and serve as the source domains of other processes. Many other processes can be modeled on material processes. For example:

(61) (a) Leaves have fallen to the ground.
(b) The temperature *has fallen* to 26° below zero.
(c) ?

(62) (a) The snow soon melted away.
(b) His followers *melted away* at the first sight of danger.
(c) His followers left him at the first sight of danger.

(63) (a) Not an apple fell from the tree.
(b) Not a word *fell* from his lips.
(c) He did not speak one word.

(64) (a) The spot of water evaporated in the sun.
(b) His anger *evaporated* (as the misunderstanding was explained away).
(c) He was no longer angry (as the misunderstanding was explained away).

In the examples above, both (a) and (b) are in material processes, but (a) is nonmetaphorical and (b) is metaphorical since (a) is the stereotype expressions of material processes and (b) is not; (a) serves as the prototype for (b). The metaphorical material processes of (b) are chosen to express the meaning of an abstract entity process in (61)(c), that of a behavioural process in (62) (c), that of a verbal process in (63)(c) and that of a relational process in (64) (c). Though material processes usually involve an inanimate object as the Actor, none of the (b) sentences have an inanimate Subject implying an object Actor. While (62)(b) has an animate Subject denoting human beings, (61)(b), (63)(b) and (64)(b) each have an inanimate Subject denoting an abstract Actor. Therefore, these metaphorical sentences are represented by the incongruent relationship between the Subject and the verb.

Besides cross-process mappings, there are intra-process mappings between material processes in their Subject-verb transitivity systems. Sentences (55)-(57) in Chapter Two are good examples. The following is another example:

(65) (a) A boat floated on the river.
(b) Leaves *floated* down from the tree.
(c) Leaves fell down from the tree.

3.2.2. Sensuous Processes

In sensuous processes, there is an animate especially a human Senser which is usually represented by the Subject. So, if a sensuous process does not have an animate Senser represented by the Subject, it is a metaphorical sentence. Look at the following examples.

(66) (a) He found Christine knitting in her room.
(b) Dusk *found* the boy crying in the street.
(c) The boy cried at dusk in the street.

(67) (a) I found her a very agreeable, sensible woman.
(b) Oliver Twist's ninth birthday *found* him still a pale and thin child.
(c) On his ninth birthday, Oliver Twist was still pale and thin.

In the two examples, the (b) sentences, which involve an incongruent relationship between the Subject and the verb, are in metaphorical sensuous processes. They are modeled on the (a) sentences respectively and encoded to realize the meaning of a behavioural process in (66)(c) and that of a relational process in (67)(c).

3.2.3 Behavioural Processes

The behavioural process may be assumed as the earliest process of transitivity systems. It is very useful in expressing man's experience. In many cases we may know a thing at first glance by scanning its superficial feature and obvious behaviour. Therefore, behavioural process may be a metaphorizing pattern. For instance:

(68) (a) A lone gull flew across the sky.
(b) The train *flew* past the station.
(c) The train moved past the station rapidly.

(69) (a) The doctor visited Beijing last year.
(b) The plague *visited* London in 1665.
(c) The plague happened in London in 1665.

(70) (a) He came into the room.

(b) A wonderful sight *came into* Mary's view.

(c) Mary saw something wonderful.

(71) (a) She came to me at once.

(b) A good idea *came to* Mary's mind.

(c) Mary thought of a good idea.

(72) (a) Jack came to Shanghai yesterday.

(b) Reports *came* to Jordan that Iraq had ordered general mobilization.

(c) It was reported in Jordan that Iraq had ordered general mobilization.

(73) (a) A child stood near the door.

(b) A bed *stood* near the wall.

(c) There was a bed near the wall.

In the examples above, the (b) sentences are all in metaphorical behavioural processes. They are modeled on the (a) sentences respectively and incorporated to express the meaning of a material process in (68)(c), that of an abstract entity process in (69)(c) and that of a sensuous process in (70)(c). (71)(c) is in a mental process, (72)(c) in a verbal process, and (73)(c) in an existential process.

Besides cross-process mappings, there are intra-process mappings between behavioural processes in their Subject-verb transitivity systems. There are many examples in Chapter Two such as (2) – (6). Here is another example:

(74) (a) A bird flew across the sky.

(b) He *flew* to tell them the news.

(c) He ran to tell them the news

3.2.4 Mental Processes

Mental processes are processes of thinking, which normally require a human Thinker. But mental activity has been a mystery to man. He can feel it but can scarcely make clear how it functions. In other words, mental processes are abstract. Therefore, mental processes seldom function as prototypes for other processes, but often serve as the models of other processes. However, this does not mean that a mental process cannot serve as the prototype for other processes. It may be the prototype for abstract entity processes and behavioural processes. For example:

(75) (a) I suppose him to be in the office.
(b) An invention supposes an inventor.
(c) ?

(76) (a) Tom thought the book worth publication.
(b) The crow thinks her own bird fairest.
(c) ?

Besides cross-process mappings, there are intra-process mappings between mental processes in their Subject-verb transitivity systems. Here is an example:

(77) (a) He does not agree with his father.
(b) My understanding of the word does not *agree with* you.
(c) I understand the word differently from yours.

In (77), all the three sentences are in mental processes, but (a) and (c) are nonmetaphorical while (b) is metaphorical since (b) involves an incongruent relationship between the Subject and the verb.

(b) is modeled on (a) in structure and encoded to express the meaning of (c).

3.2.5 Verbal Processes

Verbal processes are those of saying. They typically involve a human Sayer represented by the Subject. If a verbal process does not have a human Sayer, it is a metaphorical sentence. For example:

(78) (a) She said a few words.
(b) The clock *says* twelve.
(c) The clock strikes twelve.

(79) (a) (She knows who did it, but) she won't tell.
(b) Every blow *tells*.
(c) ?

(80) (a) I'll tell you if I'll go or not.
(b) Time will *tell* if we have been successful.
(c) We'll know if we have been successful after some time.

(81) (a) My friends tell me that you've been unwell.
(b) The sound of Sir Henry Clinton's cannon told Stirling that the enemy was between him and the lines.
(c) Judging from the sound of Sir Henry Clinton's cannon, Stirling knew that the enemy was between him and the lines.

(82) (a) We spoke about the need of economy.
(b) The book *speaks* about the writer's childhood.
(c) The book is about the writer's childhood.

In the examples above, the (b) sentences are all in metaphorical verbal processes since the Sayers are not human. They are used metaphorically to express the meaning of a material process in (78)(c) and that of an abstract entity process in (79)(c). (80)(c) and (81)(c) are in mental processes and (82)(c) is in a relational process.

3.2.6 Relational Processes

Though the relational process type is established comparatively later than some other process types, its potential power in representing man's experience is inexhaustible. Many researchers assume that it originated from the primitives' consciousness of the relationship between two or more corresponding things, and then a thing and its features. The lack of copular verb in many ancient languages (and still many modern languages) enabled the speakers to connect together two things directly or indirectly.

The universality of the relational process makes it one of the most important structures in English, and thus a hotbed for breeding metaphorical sentences. Most other process types can be modeled on this pattern. This will be discussed further in 4.1.4 and 4.3.5.

As far as the Subject-verb transitivity systems are concerned, however, the relational processes are more restricted in mapping on other processes. Only the possessive processes can serve as source domains.

In the possessive process, the relationship between the two participants is one of ownership, that is, one entity possesses another. Therefore, the stereotype of the process may be supposed as "Human Possessor ∧ verb process ∧ Physical Possessed". When the process is worded metaphorically instead of other processes in their Subject-verb transitivity systems, it often involves a nonhuman Possessor. For example:

(83) (b) Bad news *has* wings.

(c) ?

(84) (b) The house *has* five rooms.

(c) There are five rooms in the house.

In the two examples above, possessive processes of (b) are used metaphorically to express the meaning of an abstract entity process in (83)(c) and that of an existential process in (84)(c). Note that the prototype sentences are not given.

Besides cross-process mappings and intra-process mappings, some processes may also be used metaphorically to encode the meaning of complex sentences. For instance:

(85) (a) A scientist never presupposes the truth of an unproved fact.

(b) Sound sleep *presupposes* a peaceful mind.

(c) If one sleeps soundly, one has a peaceful mind.

(86) (a) They prevented him from working on the following day.

(b) His fear of losing *prevented* him from entering.

(c) Because he was afraid of losing, he did not enter.

(87) (a) Juliana came with her classmates in the morning.

(b) The biggest excitement *came* with the news late in 1775.

(c) They became incomparably excited when they heard the news late in 1775.

In the examples above, all the (b) sentences are metaphorical. While (85)(b) is in a mental process, (86)(b) and (87)(b) are in behavioural processes. They are used to express the meaning of the complex sentences in (c). While mental processes stereotypically require a human Thinker represented by the Subject and behavioural processes require an animate especially a human Behaver represented by the Subject, none of the (b) sentences meet the requirement. They all have a Subject implying an abstract entity, so they are metaphorical sentences in their Subject-verb transitivity systems.

These examples seem to indicate that the processes are used to express the meaning of complex sentences by virtue of nominalization.

The notion of nominalization is a contribution made mainly by the formal grammarians. It indicates a noun phrase which "has a systematic correspondence with a clause structure". It is "normally related morphologically to a verb" or "to an adjective" (Quirk, et al, 1985: 1288). Therefore, nominalizations are the so-called abstract nouns of action and those of property, or deverbal and deadjective nouns. However, some verbs have no corresponding deverbal nouns. In such a case, we make use of a verbal noun ending with -ing.

By nominalizing, "processes (congruently worded as verbs) and properties (congruently worded as adjectives) are reworded as nouns", so it "is the single most powerful resource" (Halliday, 1994: 352) for creating metaphorical sentences. Since *One sleeps soundly* in (85)(c) is nominalized into *sound sleep* in (85)(b)—a noun phrase that can enter a sentence as a participant, the complex sentence can be expressed in one verb process. Similarly, because *He was afraid of losing* in (86)(c) is nominalized into *his fear of losing* in (86)(b) and *They became incomparably excited* in (87)(c) is nominalized into *the biggest excitement* in (87)(b), (86)(c) and (87)(c) can be packed into one verb process in (b).

Nominalization also includes nominalized clauses, finite or nonfinite. The nominalized finite clauses are that-clauses and wh-clauses, and the nominalized nonfinite clauses are to-infinitives and -ing participles. When these clauses are embedded in another clause as the Subjects, metaphorical sentences come into being and they are represented by the Subject-verb transitivity systems. For example:

(88) That the medical technicians were available *does not make* the government's conduct any less offensive.

(89) Whatever America hopes to bring to pass in the world must first *come to pass* in the heart of Americans.

(90) It *gives* me great pleasure to be here with you.

(91) Reflecting on this and related matters *took* him past his stop.

Nominalizations may also function frequently in metaphorical sentences represented by the verb-Object and the Subject-verb-Object/Complement transitivity systems.

3.2.7 Summary

This section has given a presentation of the representation of the Subject-verb transitivity systems of metaphorical sentences in English. Six processes are discussed in detail. Most of them involve cross-process mappings while some of them contain intra-process mappings. Some of them can also be used metaphorically to realize the function of complex sentences. The representation can be summarized in Table 5:

Table 5 Representation of Subject-verb Transitivity Systems of Metaphorical Sentences in English

Source / Target	Mater. P.	AbsEnt. P.	Sens. P.	Behav. P.	Mental P.	Verbal P.	Relat. P.	Exist. P.
Mater. P.	✔			+		+		

AbsEnt. P.	+			+	+	+	+	
Sens. P.				+				
Behav. P.	+		+	✔	+			
Mental P.				+	✔	+		
Verbal P.	+			+				
Relat. P.	+		+			+		
Exist. P.				+			+	
Complex Sentence				+	+			

Key: Mater. = Material, AbsEnt. = Abstract Entity, Sens. = Sensuous, Behav. = Behavioural, Relat. = Relational, Exist. = Existential, P. = Process, + = cross mapping, ✔ = intra-mapping

Table 5 shows that there are six source domains of processes. They are material, sensuous, behavioural, mental, verbal and relational processes. The behavioural process is the most commonly used source domain. It can be mapped onto all the other processes except the relational processes. Material processes and verbal processes are another two commonly used source domains. Moreover, material processes, behavioural processes and mental processes can serve as the source domains of other material processes, behavioural processes and mental processes respectively. Besides this, behavioural processes and mental processes may be used metaphorically to express the meaning of complex sentences.

While the source domain consists of six process types, the target domain is wider. It includes not only the eight process types but also complex sentences. Abstract entity processes are the most commonly used target domains. They can be incongruently realized by material processes, behavioural processes, mental processes, verbal processes and relational processes.

3.3 Representation of Subject-verb Transitivity Systems of Metaphorical Sentences in Chinese

The preceding section has presented a study of the representation of English metaphorical sentences in their Subject-verb transitivity systems. This section will discuss the representation of Chinese metaphorical sentences in their Subject-verb transitivity systems.

As discussed in Chapter Two, the Chinese language is full of metaphorical sentences, which are generated via different mechanisms of metaphorization from one or one kind of thing to another, usually from the concrete and physical to the abstract and nonphysical. As far as the processes are concerned, the metaphorical mappings are also from those of concrete and physical entities to those of abstract and nonphysical entities. Therefore, abstract entity processes in Chinese are also commonly modeled on other processes and realized metaphorically without the congruent forms. These are the designatory metaphors. Consider the following two examples about time, which are both modeled on the behavioural processes. In order to save space, the prototype sentences are omitted.

(92) 严冬就要*来临*。
(93) 这十天很快就*过去*了。

Though Chinese metaphorical sentences share some similarities with English in their metaphorical mappings of the transitivity systems from those of concrete and physical entities to those of abstract and nonphysical entities, there are differences in their representation of the transitivity systems, especially in the relationship between the Subject and the verb. In Chinese, there is a clearcut distinction between animate verbs and inanimate verbs. Some process types generally involve an animate participant, especially a human participant as the Senser, the Behaver, the Thinker and the Sayer. Specifically, they are the sensuous process, the behavioural process, the mental process and the verbal process. Generally speaking, sentences which contain these processes need animate Subjects, especially human Subjects. Inanimate Subjects, as a rule, are prohibited in such sentences. Therefore, these process types are seldom used metaphorically to express the meaning of other process types in their Subject-verb transitivity systems. However, this does not mean that all the process types in Chinese cannot be used metaphorically to express the meaning of other processes in their Subject-verb transitivity systems. Material processes, behavioural processes and verbal processes can all be projected onto other processes.

3.3.1 Material Processes

Material processes in Chinese, besides intra-process mappings, can be projected onto abstract entity processes, behavioural processes and relational processes in their Subject-verb transitivity systems. For example:

(94) (a) 一支小船漂浮在水面上。

(b) 一盏盏航标灯*漂浮*在水面上。

(c) 一盏盏航标灯闪耀在水面上。

(95) (a) 那座大坝垮了。

(b) 他的精神*垮*了。

(c) ?

(96) (a) 小河里的水都流到大海里去了。

(b) 人才应该*流动*到最需要的地方去。

(c) 人才应该到最需要的地方去。

(97) (a) 全部玻璃窗都碎了。

(b) 她的心都*碎*了。

(c) 她很悲伤。

In the examples above, all the (b) sentences are modeled on (a), which are in material processes. Actually, these metaphorical material processes are used incongruently to express the meaning of another material process in (94)(c), that of a behavioural process in (95)(c) and that of a relational process in (97)(c). (95)(c) should be in an abstract entity process. All the (b) sentences involve an incongruent relationship between the Subject and the verb.

3.3.2 Behavioural Processes

Behavioural processes in Chinese, besides intra-process mappings, can serve as prototypes for material processes, abstract entity processes and relational processes. Their transference into material processes can be exemplified by (65) – (68) in Chapter Two. Their mappings on abstract entity processes can be illustrated by (92) and (93) above. The following is an example of projecting a behavioural process onto a relational process:

(98) (a) 如果嫂夫人允许的话，我一定亲自到府上拜访。

(b) 如果时间*允许*的话，我一定去看你。

(c) 如果有时间的话，我一定去看你。

The intra-process mappings of behavioural processes can be evidenced by (58) – (64), (75) – (78) and (88) – (90) in Chapter Two.

3.3.3 Verbal Processes

Verbal processes in Chinese can seldom serve as prototypes for other processes in their Subject-verb transitivity systems, but this does not mean that they cannot play such a role. The following translation of Mao Dun's serves as a very good example:

(99) And everything, everything in the house—the kitchen table with the round black marks of hot iron pots, the green washstand with the white daisies painted on it, the cupboard with the cups from which no one ever drank, the dark pictures on the wall—everything *spoke of* a long life that had been lived in this now tenantless house, of the granddad and granny, of the children who pored over their textbooks at the table, of quiet winter and summer evenings. (*The People Immortal*)

里面每一件物件，屋子里每一件物件——曾被灼热的铁壶烫起了圆的黑印的厨房里的桌子，有白色雏菊的绿色的洗脸台，放着从没有人用过的杯子的杯碟橱，挂在墙头的旧画片——这一切物件都*诉说*了这一座现在没有人住的屋子有过如何久长的历史，都*诉说*了乃祖考妣以至在桌上留下了他们的教科书的孙儿们曾经如何生活于斯，曾经度过了多少安静的严冬炎夏的黄昏。(《不朽的人民》)

In this example, the verbal process does not have a human Sayer, so it is a metaphorical sentence, which is represented by the

Subject-verb transitivity system. It is used to express the meaning of a behavioural process, but the congruent behavioural process is really difficult to provide, which may be the reason why Mao Dun still uses an incongruent verbal process in his translation.

The representation of Chinese metaphorical sentences in Subject-verb transitivity systems is briefly displayed in Table 6:

Table 6 Representation of Subject-verb Transitivity Systems of Metaphorical Sentences in Chinese

Source / Target	Mater. P.	AbsEnt. P.	Sens. P.	Behav. P.	Mental P.	Verbal P.	Relat. P.	Exist. P.
Mater. P.	✔			+				
AbsEnt. P.	+			+				
Sens. P.								
Behav. P.	+			✔		+		
Mental P.								
Verbal P.								
Relat. P.	+			+				
Exist. P.								
Complex Sentence								

Key: Mater. = Material, AbsEnt. = Abstract Entity, Sens. = Sensuous, Behav. = Behavioural, Relat. = Relational, Exist. = Existential, P. = Process, + = cross mapping, ✔ = intra-mapping

Table 6 shows that there are three source domains and four target domains in the representation of the Subject-verb transitivity systems of Chinese metaphorical sentences. The source domains are the material, the behavioural and the verbal processes. Material and behavioural processes are the more commonly used source domains. They involve both cross-process mappings and intra-process mappings. The target domains are the material process, the abstract entity process, the behavioural process and the relational process.

In summary, both English and Chinese metaphorical sentences can be represented by the incongruent relationship between the Subject and the verb. But English metaphorical sentences seem to concern more process types in both the source domains and the target domains. While English metaphorical sentences involve six process types as the source domains and seven process types as the target domains, Chinese metaphorical sentences just involve three process types as the source domains and four process types as the target domains. Moreover, cross-process metaphorical sentences seem to be numerous in English, but they are very few in Chinese, excepting the metaphorical expressions of abstract entities in other processes. The Chinese sentences given in the last section seem to be the only few examples. However, intra-process mappings within material and behavioural processes seem to be as abundant in Chinese as in English.

Chapter Four

Representation of verb-Object and Subject-verb-Object/Complement Transitivity Systems of Metaphorical Sentences in English and Chinese

Chapter Three has been devoted to the representation of Subject-verb transitivity systems in metaphorical sentences in English and Chinese. This chapter will deal with the representation of verb-Object and Subject-verb-Object/Complement transitivity systems in metaphorical sentences in the two languages.

4.1 Representation of verb-Object Transitivity Systems of Metaphorical Sentences in English

In English, many process types involve two participants, so they may be worded in SVO sentence pattern. When these processes are used metaphorically, they may involve an incongruent relationship between the verb and the Object. These process types include the material process, the sensuous process, the behavioural process and the relational process. They will be discussed one after another.

4.1.1 Material Processes

Besides an inanimate physical Actor, material processes sometimes involve a physical Goal. When the Goal is not physical, the process is used metaphorically, and the metaphorical sentence is represented by the incongruent relationship between the verb and the Object. For example:

(1) (a) An atom bomb destroyed the city.
(b)A heavy rain *destroyed* my plan.
(c) ?

(2) (a) The wind broke some branches of the tree.
(b) The bushes *broke* his fall (or he would have been killed).
(c) He fell on the bushes (or he would have been killed).

In the examples above, both the (b) sentences are in metaphorical material processes, which involve nonphysical entities represented by the Objects. They are incorporated to express the meaning of an abstract entity process in (1)(c) and a behavioural process in (2)(c).

4.1.2 Sensuous Processes

In addition to an animate Senser, a sensuous process usually involves another participant of the Phenomenon, which should be physical. Otherwise, the Phenomenon cannot be sensed directly. However, when the sensuous processes are mapped on other processes metaphorically, they may involve a nonphysical Phenomenon. Namely, the metaphorical sentence is represented by an incongruent realization of the verb-Object transitivity systems. For example:

(3) (a) Sophia saw the famous star herself.
(b) I *see* what you mean.
(c) I know what you mean.

(4) (a) She was smelling the flowers.
(b) Mary can *smell* trouble a mile away.
(c) Mary can guess trouble a mile away.

In the two examples above, the congruent mental processes of (c) are incongruently realized by the sensuous processes in (b), which are modeled on (a). Nevertheless, neither of the (b) sentences has a physical Phenomenon.

4.1.3 Behavioural Processes

Besides the Behaver, behavioural processes sometimes involve another participant of the Patient, which should be physical. But when behavioural processes are used metaphorically instead of other processes, they often contain a nonphysical Patient. In other words, the metaphorical sentences are represented by the incongruent relationship between the verb and the Object. For example:

(5) (a) Philip lost his wallet.
(b) He *lost* <u>his eyesight</u>.
(c) He couldn't see.
(6) (a) Mary never gave boys gifts.
(b) I never *gave* these things <u>a thought</u>.
(c) I never thought of these things.
(7) (a) The workers made no toys this month.
(b) Winterbourne *made* <u>no answer</u> to the question.
(c) Winterbourne did not answer the question.
(8) (a) He didn't meet his father in the station.
(b) He didn't *meet* <u>the qualifications</u>.
(c) He was not qualified.

In the examples above, the (b) sentences are all in behavioural processes. They are modeled on (a) respectively and used incongruently to express the meaning of a sensuous process in (5)(c), that of a mental process in (6)(c), that of a verbal process in (7)(c) and that of a relational process in (8)(c). They each involve an incongruent relationship between the verb and the Object.

When behavioural processes are used metaphorically in the

verb-Object transitivity systems, they are often engaged in mapping onto the mental processes. The following are some more examples:

(9) (a) They take a lot of flowers.

(b) (I don't think) she *took* my meaning.

(c) (I don't think) she understood me.

(10) (a) They put a book on the table.

(b) He *put* the height of the mountain at 5000 feet above the sea.

(c) He thought that the height of the mountain was at 5000 feet above the sea.

(11) (a) The PLA men established a hospital in my hometown after liberation.

(b) The police cannot *establish* where he was at that time.

(c) The police cannot judge where he was at that time.

Besides cross-process mappings, there are intra-process mappings between behavioural processes in the representation of verb-Object transitivity systems. While the verb processes in the following examples are all behavioural, (b) is the incongruent realization but (c) is the congruent. Though all the verb processes require a physical Patient represented by the Object, none of the (b) sentences fulfill the requirement. Note that the prototype sentences are omitted, because it is difficult to find suitable ones.

(12) (b) My friend *did* some cooking.

(c) My friend cooked.

(13) (b) She *gave* me a push.

(c) She pushed me.

(14) (b) Lenin *made* a careful study of Marx's works.

(c) Lenin studied Marx's works carefully.

(15) (b) They *took* a drive in the country.

(c) They drove in the country.

The examples above seem to show that the behavioural process serves as prototypes for metaphorical mappings in their verb-Object transitivity systems by virtue of nominalizations and the structure of empty verbs, such as *do*, *give*, *make* and *take*. In this structure, "the verb is lexically empty", so Halliday maintains that "the process of the clause is expressed only by the noun"(Halliday, 1994: 147). Then *make a pan* and *make a fan*, for example, are no doubt behavioural processes, but *make a pun* has to be analyzed as a verbal process though the three processes contain the same verb *make*. This analysis will make things confusing. Therefore, the author finds it more reasonable to label all the three processes as behavioural. The first two are the congruent realization of the behavioural processes and the third one is the metaphorical realization of the behavioural process. In other words, the third one is the model of the behavioural process.

The nominalizations here usually involve the abstract nouns of action.

4.1.4 Relational Processes

As in the representation of the Subject-verb transitivity systems, only possessive relational processes can serve as prototypes for other processes and be used metaphorically in the verb-Object transitivity systems. Many other processes can be patterned upon possessive processes. In order to save space, the prototype sentences are omitted in the following examples. Only the metaphorical sentences and their synonymous sentences are listed.

(16) (b) She *has* a dislike for him.
(c) She dislikes him.
(17) (b) She *had* a good cry over that letter.
(c) She cried hard over that letter.
(18) (b) I still *have* my doubts about his honesty.
(c) I still doubt his honesty.
(19) (b) They *are having* an argument.
(c)They are arguing.

In these examples, all the (b) sentences are in metaphorical possessive processes. They are used to express the meaning of a sensuous process in (16)(c) and that of a behavioural process in (17)(c). (18)(c) is in a mental process, and (19)(c) is in a verbal process. While possessive processes usually involve a physical Possessed, none of the (b) sentences fulfill this requirement.

In analyzing these metaphorical processes, one thing should be kept in mind that *have* is also one of the empty verbs in English. It is treated in the same way as other empty verbs in 4.1.3.

The relational: possessive subtype can also be the source domain for the other subtypes of relational processes. The intensive process is the one that is always patterned upon this prototype. This can be exemplified as follows:

(20) (b) He *has* no patience with me.
(c) He is not patient with me.
(21) (b) He *had* a pale look.
(c) He looked pale.

The representation of English metaphorical sentences in their verb-Object transitivity systems can be summarized in Table 7 on Page 113:

Table 7 Representation of verb-Object Transitivity Systems of Metaphorical Sentences in English

Source / Target	Mater. P.	AbsEnt . P.	Sens. P.	Behav. P.	Mental P.	Verbal P.	Relat. P.	Exist. P.
Mater. P.								
AbsEnt. P.	+							
Sens. P.				+			+	
Behav. P.	+			✔			+	
Mental P.			+	+			+	
Verbal P.				+			+	
Relat. P.				+			✔	
Exist. P.								
Complex Sentence								

Key: Mater. = Material, AbsEnt. = Abstract Entity, Sens. = Sensuous, Behav. = Behavioural, Relat. = Relational, Exist. = Existential, P. = Process, + = cross mapping, ✔ = intra-mapping

Table 7 shows that, in the metaphorical representation of the verb-Object transitivity systems in English, there are four source processes and six target processes. The source processes are the material, the sensuous, the behavioural and the relational processes. The target processes are the abstract entity process, the sensuous process, the behavioural process, the mental process, the verbal process and the relational process. Of the four source domains, behavioural and relational processes are more often used. They may involve both cross-process mappings and intra-process mappings. Of the target domains, mental processes are more commonly used. They can be patterned on the sensuous, the behavioural and the relational processes.

4.2 Representation of verb-Object Transitivity Systems of Metaphorical Sentences in Chinese

As in English, many process types in Chinese involve two participants, so they may be worded in SVO sentence pattern. When these processes are used metaphorically, they may involve an incongruent relationship between the verb and the Object. These process types include the sensuous process, the behavioural process and the relational process. They will be discussed in this section one after another.

4.2.1 Sensuous Processes

As in English, a sensuous process in Chinese usually involves two participants, an animate Senser and a physical Phenomenon. However, when sensuous processes are mapped onto other processes metaphorically, they may involve a nonphysical Phenomenon. Namely, the metaphorical sentence is represented by an incongruent realization of verb-Object transitivity systems. For example:

(22) (a) 我尝遍了各种水果。

(b) (在旧社会，)他*尝尽*了人间的艰辛。

(c) (在旧社会，)他经历了无数的艰辛。

(23) (b) *回顾*过去

(c) 回忆过去

In the two examples above, the sensuous processes in (b) are used metaphorically to express the meaning of a behavioural process in (22) (c) and a mental process in (23) (c). Nevertheless, neither of the (b) sentences has an Object implying a physical Phenomenon.

Note that the prototype sentence for (23)(b) is not given, because *回顾* (look backward at) is now mainly used with abstract Object. In other words, it has undergone a semantic change via metaphorization.

4.2.2 Behavioural Processes

Chinese behavioural processes may involve two participants, usually an animate especially a human Behaver and a physical Patient. But when a behavioural process is used incongruently to express the meaning of other processes, it contains a nonphysical Patient. Therefore, the metaphorical sentence is represented by the incongruent verb-Object transitivity system. For example:

(24) (a) 每个人都得到一份礼物。
(b) 他终于*得到*了大家的原谅。
(c) 大家终于原谅他了。
(25) (a) 要用一段时间来消化食物。
(b) 要用一段时间来*消化*这些知识。
(c) 要用一段时间来理解这些知识。
(26) (a) 他正在给我倒着水呢。
(b) 她正在给我*倒*着肚子里的委屈。
(c) 她正在给我诉说着肚子里的委屈。

In these examples, all the (b) sentences are in metaphorical behavioural processes. They are modeled on (a) respectively and used incongruently to realize the meaning of a sensuous process in (24)(c), that of a mental process in (25)(c) and that of a verbal process in (26)(c). They all involve a metaphorical realization of the relationship between the verb and the Object.

As in English, behavioural processes in Chinese can also be metaphorically used in their verb-Object transitivity systems through the structure of empty verbs. Chinese empty verbs include 加以，给以，予以，给予，进行 and 作（胡裕树、范晓，1995：265）. Consider the following examples.

(27) (b) 我的申请，请领导*予以*考虑。
(c) 请领导考虑我的申请。

(28) (b) 记者们提出的问题，部长都一一*作*了回答。
(c) 部长一一回答了记者们提出的问题。

The (b) sentences above are both in metaphorical behavioural processes. They are metaphorized through the use of the empty verbs 予以 and 作. They are used to express the meaning of a mental process in (27)(c) and that of a verbal process in (28)(c). They both involve an incongruent relationship between the verb and the Object. Stereotypically, a behavioural process requires a physical Patient represented by the Object, but the Objects in the (b) sentences both imply human behaviour realized by nominalized verbs. Note that the prototype sentences are not given, because it is difficult to find suitable ones.

Besides cross-process mappings, there are intra-process mappings between behavioural processes in their incongruent realization of the verb-Object transitivity systems by virtue of empty verbs. For instance:

(29) (b) 敌人对她*进行*威胁。
(c) 敌人威胁她。

(30) (b) 我们要对这件事*进行*认真的调查。

(c) 我们要认真调查这件事。

Though Chinese behavioural processes in their verb-Object transitivity systems can be mapped on many other processes, they usually serve as the prototypes for mental processes. Here are some more examples:

(31) (a) 他们总是扔不掉这只小狗。

(b) 我总是*扔不掉*这个念头。

(c) 我总是忘不了这个念头。

(32) (a) 他陷入泥潭。

(b) 她*陷入*了对往事的回忆。

(c) 她回想起了往事。

4.2.3 Relational Processes

As in English, only the possessive relational process in Chinese can be used metaphorically in the verb-Object transitivity systems. When the process is worded incongruently instead of other processes, it involves a nonphysical Possessed. Therefore, the metaphorical sentence is represented by an incongruent relationship between the verb and the Object.

Almost all the other processes can be modeled upon the relational possessive process. In order to save space, the prototype sentences are omitted in the following examples. Only the metaphorical sentences and their synonymous ones are listed.

(33) (b) 他*有*爱*有*恨。

(c) 他又爱又恨。

(34) (b) 我们也*有*准备。

(c) 我们也准备了。

(35) (b) 我们不能再*有*丝毫的疑惑了。

(c) 我们不能再疑惑了。

(36) (b) 他*有*说*有*笑。

(c) 他又说又笑。

In these examples, all the (b) sentences are in metaphorical possessive processes, since they involve a nonphysical Object. They are used to realize the meaning of sensuous processes in (33)(c) and that of a behavioural process in (34)(c). (35)(c) is in a mental process and (36)(c) contains a verbal process and a behavioural process.

The possessive subtype can also be the source domain for the other subtypes of relational processes. The intensive process is one that is often patterned upon this prototype. This can be exemplified by the following example:

(37) (b) 她一天到晚总*有*那么多忧愁。

(c) 她一天到晚总是那么忧愁。

The representation of Chinese metaphorical sentences in their verb-Object transitivity systems can be summarized in Table 8:

Table 8 shows that, in the metaphorical representation of the verb-Object transitivity systems in Chinese, there are three source processes and five target processes. The source processes are the sensuous, the behavioural and the relational processes. The target processes are the sensuous, the behavioural, the mental, the verbal and the relational processes. Of the three source domains, relational and behavioural processes are more often used. They involve both cross-process mappings and intra-process mappings. Of the target domains, mental processes are more commonly used. They can be models of the sensuous, the behavioural and the relational processes.

Table 8 Representation of verb-Object Transitivity Systems of Metaphorical Sentences in Chinese

Source / Target	Mater. P.	AbsEnt. P.	Sens. P.	Behav. P.	Mental P.	Verbal P.	Relat. P.	Exist. P.
Mater. P.								
AbsEnt. P.								
Sens. P.				+			+	
Behav. P.			+	✔			+	
Mental P.			+	+			+	
Verbal P.				+			+	
Relat. P.							✔	
Exist. P.								
Complex Sentence								

Key: Mater. = Material, AbsEnt. = Abstract Entity, Sens. = Sensuous, Behav. = Behavioural, Relat. = Relational, Exist. = Existential, P. = Process, + = cross mapping, ✔ = intra-mapping

In summary, both English and Chinese metaphorical sentences can be represented by verb-Object transitivity systems. Behavioural processes and relational processes in both English and Chinese involve inter-process mappings as well as intra-process mappings. Moreover, in both English and Chinese only possessive relational processes are involved metaphorically in verb-Object transitivity systems. However, there are some differences between English and Chinese metaphorical sentences in their verb-Object transitivity systems. Firstly, there are more source domains and target domains in English than in Chinese. While there are four source processes and six target processes in English, there are only three sources and five targets in Chinese. Secondly, while English sensuous processes can only serve as prototypes for mental processes, Chinese sensuous processes can be source domains of behavioural processes as well as mental processes. Thirdly, while Chinese behavioural processes can only be projected onto sensuous, mental and verbal processes, English behavioural processes can be mapped on sensuous, mental, verbal and relational processes. Finally, while English behavioural processes usually map on other processes through empty verbs, Chinese behavioural processes may project on other processes either directly or with the help of empty verbs.

4.3 Representation of Subject-verb-Object/ Complement Transitivity Systems of Metaphorical Sentences in English

As discussed above, English metaphorical sentences can be represented by an incongruent realization of the relationship between either the Subject and the verb or the verb and the Object. They can naturally be represented by a metaphorical realization of the relationship between both the Subject and the verb on the one hand, and the verb and the Object on the other hand, or simply put, the Subject-verb-Object relationship. The process types involved in this kind of representation include the material process, the sensuous process, the behavioural process, the verbal process, the relational process and the existential process. Since relational processes are also often worded in SVC sentence pattern, they may involve an incongruent realization of Subject-verb-Complement transitivity systems. For the convenience of discussion, the Subject-verb-Complement transitivity system is discussed together with the Subject-verb-Object transitivity system.

Many processes are used metaphorically via nominalizations in their Subject-verb-Object/Complement transitivity systems.

4.3.1 Material Processes

In English, some material processes involve two participants, a physical Actor and a physical Goal. These processes are usually worded in SVO pattern. When the verb processes have an incongruent relationship with both the Actor and · the Goal, a metaphorical sentence emerges. In other words, the metaphorical sentence is represented by an incongruent Subject-verb-Object transitivity system. For example:

(38) (a) The sun melted the snow.
(b) His pleading *melted* her.
(c) She yielded to his pleading.

In this example, (a) is the prototype and (b) is the model, so they are both in material processes. But (b) is metaphorical and is used to express the meaning of the behavioural process in (c). While the verb process *melt* requires a hot object as the Actor and a meltable object as the Goal, neither is fulfilled by sentence (b).

Material processes may also be used metaphorically to realize the meaning of a complex sentence. For example:

(39) (a) The path leads to the river.
(b) Our hard training *led to* our winning in the game.
(c) Because we trained hard, we won the game.

4.3.2 Sensuous Processes

When sensuous processes are used metaphorically in the representation of the Subject-verb-Object transitivity systems, they are usually mapped on abstract entity processes and behavioural processes. For example:

(40) (a) I saw him in the city.
(b) 1980 *saw* great changes in Guangzhou.
(c) Great changes took place in Guangzhou in 1980.

(41) (a) We saw them on the bus.
(b) The fifth day *saw* their ascent on the mountain.
(c) They climbed the mountain on the fifth day.

In the examples above, sensuous processes are used as prototypes to realize the meaning of an abstract entity process in (40)(c) and a behavioural process in (41)(c). In the metaphorical sensuous processes, both the Senser and the Phenomenon are abstracts. Therefore, they involve an incongruent realization of the Subject-verb-Object transitivity systems.

Besides mapping on abstract entity processes and behavioural processes, a sensuous process can be incorporated to realize the function of a complex sentence. For instance:

(42) (b) Pit closures *saw* violent protests.
(c) The Coal Board closed 30 pits, so miners protested.

4.3.3 Behavioural Processes

In English, some behavioural processes involve two participants, an animate especially a human Behaver and a physical object Patient. These processes are usually worded in SVO sentence pattern. When the verb processes have an incongruent relationship with both the Behaver and the Patient, there arises a metaphorical sentence. In other words, the metaphorical sentence is represented by an incongruent Subject-verb-Object relationship. For example:

(43) (a) Mother (opened the gate and) let in the dog.

(b) The roof *let in* the rain.

(c) The roof leaked.

(44) (a) I depend on you (for a proper understanding of the country).

(b) The price *depends on* the quality.

(c) ?

(45) (a) The police caught the thief.

(b) A flash of colour *caught* her eye.

(c) She saw a flash of colour.

(46) (a) He struck the nail with a hammer.

(b) An awful thought has just *struck* me.

(c) I've just thought of an awful thought.

(47) (a) The workers produce more than 200 cars this month.

(b) The morrow *produces* no abatement of Mrs Bennet's ill humour and ill health.

(c) The next day Mrs Bennet was still in ill humour and ill health.

(48) (a) The child followed her mother about all day long.
(b) Applause *followed* his singing of a song.
(c) After he sang a song, the audience applauded.

In these examples, the (b) sentences are all in metaphorical behavioural processes. They are modeled on (a) respectively and used to express the meaning of a material process in (43)(c), that of a sensuous process in (45)(c) and that of a mental process in (46)(c). (47)(c) is in a relational process and (48)(c) is a complex sentence. (44)(c) should be in an abstract entity process, which is difficult to encode.

Besides cross-domain mappings, one behavioural process can serve as the prototype for another behavioural process. For instance:

(49) (a) He upset the teapot.
(b) The war *upset* all their plans.
(c) They couldn't carry out their plans because of the war.

4.3.4 Verbal Processes

Verbal processes can be used metaphorically to express the meaning of complex sentences in their Subject-verb-Object transitivity systems. For instance:

(50) (a) He speaks French.
(b) Something about the bird *spoke* Charles Ives.
(c) If one saw the bird, he somehow thought of Charles Ives.

In this example, the verbal process is encoded to realize the function of a complex sentence. However, the verb group *speak* has undergone semantic expanding, so people seldom notice that it is a metaphor.

4.3.5 Relational Processes

In relational processes, the relationship between the two participants is usually one between the classified and the class it belongs to or between the identified and its identity (范晓, 1996: 370). But in the metaphorical relational processes, the same is no longer true of the relationship between the two participants. In other words, there is not a congruent relationship between the two participants. Therefore, the metaphorical realization of the relational processes is represented by the incongruent Subject-verb-Complement transitivity systems. For example:

(51) (b) His love for her *was* deep.
(c) He loved her deeply.
(52) (b) His treatment of the prisoners *was* very generous.
(c)He treated the prisoners very generously.
(53) (b) This event *was* beyond Philip's knowledge.
(c) Philip did not know this event.
(54) (b) His strange behaviour *was* the talk of the town.
(c) All the people in the town talked about his strange behaviour.
(55) (b) A year *has* twelve months.
(c)There are twelve months in a year.

In these examples, all the (b) sentences are modeled on relational processes, which are omitted in order to save space. These metaphorical relational processes are used to realize the function of a sensuous process in (51)(c), that of a behavioural process in (52)(c) and that of a mental process in (53)(c). (54)(c) is in a verbal process and (55)(c) in an existential process, which is also metaphorical.

Besides cross-process mappings, one subtype of the relational processes can also be mapped on another. This often involves mapping a possessive subtype on the intensive subtype. For example:

(56) (b) The mountain in the distance *had* the appearance of glass.

(c) The mountain in the distance looked like glass.

(57) (b) The city *has* its share of modern tawdriness.

(c) The city is tawdry like other modern things.

Relational processes can also be used metaphorically to encode the meaning of complex sentences in the Subject-verb-Complement transitivity systems. For instance:

(58) (b) The reason for the accepting of Tom *was* purely his credentials.

(c) Because Tom had all the required credentials, he was accepted.

4.3.6 Existential Processes

Though existential processes are discussed here under the same topic of Subject-verb-Object transitivity systems, they are quite different from other processes since the Subject "has no representational function"(Halliday, 1994: 142). Traditionally, the Subject and the verb are treated together as one grammatical unit and the process is often labeled as "*there-be*" construction. Therefore, the existential processes, strictly speaking, may involve an incongruent realization of the Subject-verb and the Object transitivity systems. As discussed in 3.1.8, existential processes usually involve only one participant of the Existent, which should be a physical entity. If the Existent is not a physical entity, the process is used metaphorically. Or, it involves a metaphorical representation of the Subject-verb-Object transitivity systems. Existential processes may serve as prototypes for all the other processes. In order to save space, the prototype sentences are omitted in the following examples. Only the metaphorical sentences and their synonymous ones are listed.

(59) (b) There *was* an eruption of Vesuvius in 77 AD.
(c) Vesuvius erupted in 77 AD.

(60) (b) There *were* many accidents recently.
(c) Many accidents happened recently.

(61) (b)There *were* fears that there might be a power struggle among Kenyans seeking the Presidency.
(c) People feared that there might be a power struggle among Kenyans seeking the Presidency.

(62) (b) There *was* a turning away from the medieval interests.
(c) People turned away from medieval interests.

(63) (b) There *are* different views concerning the nature of perception.
(c) People view the nature of perception differently.

(64) (b) There *was* no mention of the problem.
(c) They didn't mention the problem.

(65) (b) There *is* no likeness between the two paintings.
(c) The two paintings are not alike.

All the (b) sentences in the examples above are in metaphorical existential processes, which involve an incongruent realization of the Subject-verb-Object transitivity systems. Each process contains a nonentity of the abstract action or the abstract feature as the Existent. These processes are used to realize the function of a material process in (59)(c), that of an abstract entity process in (60)(c) and that of a sensuous process in (61)(c). (62)(c) is in a behavioural process, (63)(c) is in a mental process, (64)(c) is in a verbal process and (65)(c) is in a relational process.

The representation of English metaphorical sentences in their Subject-verb-Object/Complement transitivity systems can be summarized in Table 9:

Table 9 Representation of Subject-verb-Object/Complement Transitivity Systems of Metaphorical Sentences in English

Source / Target	Mater. P.	AbsEnt. P.	Sens. P.	Behav. P.	Mental P.	Verbal P.	Relat. P.	Exist. P.
Mater. P.				+				+
AbsEnt. P.			+	+				+
Sens. P.				+			+	+
Behav. P.	+		+	✔			+	+
Mental P.				+			+	+
Verbal P.							+	+
Relat. P.				+			✔	+
Exist. P.							+	
Complex Sentence	+		+	+		+	+	

Key: Mater. = Material, AbsEnt. = Abstract Entity, Sens. = Sensuous, Behav. = Behavioural, Relat. = Relational, Exist. = Existential, P. = Process, + = cross mapping, ✔ = intra-mapping

Table 9 shows that, in the metaphorical representation of the Subject-verb-Object/Complement transitivity systems in English, there are six source domain processes and eight target domain processes. Of the source domains, behavioural, relational and existential processes are more important. Behavioural and relational processes may involve both cross-domain mappings and intra-domain mappings. Besides, material, sensuous, behavioural, verbal and relational processes can all be used metaphorically to express the meaning of complex sentences.

Of the target domains, behavioural processes are more commonly used. They can be patterned on the material, the sensuous, the relational and the existential processes.

4.4 Representation of Subject-verb-Object/ Complement Transitivity Systems of Metaphorical Sentences in Chinese

As in English, Chinese metaphorical sentences can also be represented in their Subject-verb-Object/Complement transitivity systems. The prototype processes are material processes, sensuous processes, behavioural processes, relational processes and existential processes.

4.4.1 Material Processes

When the Chinese material processes are used metaphorically in their Subject-verb-Object transitivity systems, they can be projected on sensuous processes, behavioural processes and mental processes. Examples are:

(66) (a) 官墓中埋藏着许多金银财宝。

(b) 沦陷区人民的心中深深地*埋藏着*对敌人的仇恨。

(c) 沦陷区人民十分仇恨敌人。

(67) (a) 瓶中充满了药酒。

(b) 他胸中*充满着*对旧社会的蔑视。

(c) 他非常蔑视旧社会。

(68) (a) 他的照片一直珍藏在那个樟木箱子里。

(b) 他的名字一直*珍藏在*我们一家人的心里。

(c) 我们一家人一直铭记着他的名字。

In these examples, all the (b) sentences are modeled on material processes to realize the meaning of a sensuous process in (66)(c), that of a behavioural process in (67)(c) and that of a mental process in (68)(c).

Besides cross-mappings, there are also intra-process mappings between material processes in their Subject-verb-Object transitivity systems. For instance:

(69) (a) 工厂排出的废液污染了河水。

(b) 这种"口袋书"*污染*了中学生的心灵。

(c) 这种"口袋书"使得中学生的心灵深受其害。

(70) (a) 硫酸腐蚀着玻璃。

(b) 大量的黄色书刊*腐蚀着*青年一代。

(c) 大量的黄色书刊使得青年一代深受其害。

4.4.2. Sensuous Processes

Chinese sensuous processes can be mapped on the abstract entity processes. For instance:

(71) (a) 这里的老人都目睹过佛光。

(b) 罗马城*目睹*过许多伟大的历史性事件。

(c) 罗马城发生过许多伟大的历史性事件。

4.4.3 Behavioural Processes

When the behavioural processes in Chinese are used metaphorically in their Subject-verb-Object transitivity systems, they can be projected onto the material processes and the sensuous processes. For example:

(72) (a) 山猫正在吃掉那只野兔。
(b) 铁锈正在*吃掉*小汽车。
(c) 铁锈正在腐蚀小汽车。
(73) (a) 警察很快抓住了小偷。
(b) 一种飘渺的幻灭的悲哀，在很短的一瞬间*抓住*了他的心灵。
(c) 他突然感到一种飘渺的幻灭的悲哀。

In the examples above, both (b) sentences are modeled on behavioural processes to express the meaning of a material process in (72)(c) and a sensuous process in (73)(c).

Behavioural processes can also be used incongruently to express the meaning of a complex sentence. Look at the following example:

(74) (a) 牧羊人驱散了羊群。
(b) 阳光*驱散*了她心中的沮丧。
(c) 太阳出来了，她不再沮丧。

4.4.4 Relational Processes

Chinese intensive relational processes can be worded incongruently in their Subject-verb-Complement transitivity systems. They can be mapped on the mental processes and the verbal processes.

For example:

(75) (b) 他的估计（*V*）错了。
(c) 他估计错了。
(76) (b) 这份材料*是*对穷兵黩武者的深刻的讽刺。
(c) 这份材料深刻地讽刺了穷兵黩武者。

In (75), the relational process in (b) is metaphorized to express the meaning of a mental process in (c). In (76), the verbal process in (c) is realized by a relational process in (b). The (b) sentences both involve an incongruent relationship of the Subject-verb-Complement transitivity systems. However, the verb process in (75)(b) is covert. The prototype sentences are omitted to save space.

4.4.5 Existential Processes

Chinese existential processes are different from English existential processes. Besides the Existent, they usually have a physical location represented by the Subject. When they are metaphorized in their Subject-verb-Object transitivity systems, they often involve either a nonphysical location or a nonentity Existent. They can serve as the source domains of abstract entity processes and behavioural processes. For instance:

(77) (b) 近来*有*很多车祸。
(c) 近来发生了很多车祸。
(78) (b) 他脸上*有了*笑容。
(c) 他笑了。

The representation of Chinese metaphorical sentences in their Subject-verb-Object/Complement transitivity systems can be summarized in Table 10.

Table 10 Representation of Subject-verb-Object/Complement Transitivity Systems of Metaphorical Sentences in Chinese

Source / Target	Mater. P.	AbsEnt. P.	Sens. P.	Behav. P.	Mental P.	Verbal P.	Relat. P.	Exist. P.
Mater. P.	✔			+				
AbsEnt. P.			+					+
Sens. P.	+			+				
Behav. P.	+							+
Mental P.	+						+	
Verbal P.							+	
Relat. P.								
Exist. P.								
Complex Sentence				+				

Key: Mater. = Material, AbsEnt. = Abstract Entity, Sens. = Sensuous, Behav. = Behavioural, Relat. = Relational, Exist. = Existential, P. = Process, + = cross mapping, ✔ = intra-mapping

Table 10 shows that, in the metaphorical representation of the Subject-verb-Object/Complement transitivity systems in Chinese, there are five source processes and six target processes. The source processes are the material, the sensuous, the behavioural, the relational, and the existential processes. The target processes are material processes, abstract entity processes, sensuous processes, behavioural processes, mental processes and verbal processes. Of the five source processes, material processes are more commonly used. They involve both inter- and intra- process mappings. The target domains seem to be used somewhat equally frequently.

In summary, both English and Chinese metaphorical sentences can be represented by the incongruent Subject-verb-Object/Complement transitivity systems. But English metaphorical sentences seem to involve more source domains and target domains. While English metaphorical sentences concern six prototype processes and eight model processes, Chinese metaphorical sentences only concern five prototype processes and six model processes. Moreover, while English behavioural processes can be the prototypes for five processes, Chinese behavioural processes can only be the prototypes for two processes. While English relational processes can be mapped on six processes, Chinese relational processes can only be projected onto two processes. Whereas English existential processes can serve as the source domain of seven processes, Chinese existential processes can only work as the prototype for two processes. Finally, five processes in English can be used metaphorically in the Subject-verb-Object/Complement transitivity systems to express the meaning of a complex sentence; only one process in Chinese can be thus used.

4.5 Summary and Discussion

Chapter Three and Chapter Four have presented a rather detailed study of the representation of metaphorical sentences in English and Chinese. The study shows that metaphorical sentences in both English and Chinese can be represented by incongruent Subject-verb transitivity systems, verb-Object transitivity systems and Subject-verb-Object/Complement transitivity systems. In other words, metaphorical sentences in the two languages may involve an incongruent relationship between the verb on the one hand, and the Subject, and/or the Object/Complement on the other. In each transitivity system, metaphorical sentences are represented by mapping one process or one kind of process onto another.

It seems that English and Chinese metaphorical sentences share more similarities in their representation of verb-Object transitivity systems. As for the other two transitivity systems, they seem to have more differences. This is probably because there is a clearcut distinction between animate verbs and inanimate verbs in Chinese. The animate verbs in Chinese can only be used to express animate, especially human, behaviours and doings. Therefore, the Senser, the Behaver, the Thinker and the Sayer, which are commonly realized by noun phrases as the Subject in a process, is usually a human. Other entities seldom function as the Senser, the Behaver, the Thinker or the Sayer in Chinese. However, there is no clearcut distinction between animate verbs and inanimate verbs in English. Many animate verbs have Subjects denoting inanimate entities or even abstracts. The Sayer, for example, can be "anything that puts out a signal"(Halliday, 1994: 140) in English.

In order to make clearer the contrast of English and Chinese metaphorical sentences, we'll summarize their representation in Table 11.

Table 11 Representation of Metaphorical Sentences in English and Chinese

Source / Target	Mater. P.		AbsEnt. P.		Sens. P.		Behav. P.		Mental P.		Verbal P.		Relat. P.		Exist. P.	
	E.	C.	E.	C.	E.	C.	E.	C.	E.	C.	E.	C.	E.	C.	E.	C.
Mater. P.	✔	✔					+	+			+				+	
AbsEnt. P.	+	+			+	+	+	+	+		+		+		+	+
Sens. P.		+					+	+					+	+	+	
Behav. P.	+	+			+	+	✔	✔	+			+	+	+	+	+
Mental P.		+			+	+	+	+	✔		+		+	+	+	
Verbal P.	+						+	+					+	+	+	
Relat. P.	+	+			+		+	+			+		✔	✔	+	
Exist. P.							+						+			
Complex Sentence	+				+		+	+	+		+		+			

Key: Mater. = Material, AbsEnt. = Abstract Entity, Sens. = Sensuous, Behav. = Behavioural, Relat. = Relational, Exist. = Existential, P. = Process, E. = English, C.= Chinese, + = cross mapping, ✔ = intra-mapping

Table 11 shows that both English and Chinese metaphorical sentences involve cross-domain mappings as well as intra-process mappings. The source domains are usually those of concrete behaviours, doings and happenings but not those of abstract happenings and thinking, etc. This is in accordance with the generative mechanisms of metaphorical sentences, which involve mapping concrete things on abstracts.

The most commonly used source domain is the behavioural process, which expresses the behaviours of animate beings, especially human beings. Since animate beings are the most important source domains of metaphorical mappings, so are their behaviours. The second commonly used source domain is the relational process, which expresses the relationship between two entities, particularly physical entities. Physical objects certainly provide more striking features in the human mind, so it is easy and convenient for people to map the knowledge of inanimate objects on other things. Material processes are also very commonly used as source domains. Existential processes are often encoded as prototypes in English. On the contrary, though mental processes express the goings-on of human beings, i.e., thinking, they are more subtle and abstract. They seldom function as prototypes for other processes. Actually, mental processes cannot serve as sources with a few exceptions. Generally speaking, they can only be target processes. Similarly, abstract entity processes can never be used as source domains, because they express the abstract happenings of abstract entities. However, sensuous processes seem to be intermediate. Though they express sensing of animate entities, which is available to sensory organs, affection and perception are not as concrete as behaviours. Therefore, the status of sensuous processes as source domains and target domains seems to be equal.

As different languages, English and Chinese also have their metaphorical sentences represented quite differently. Firstly, English metaphorical sentences seem to involve more source domains and target domains. While English metaphorical sentences concern seven prototype processes and eight model processes, Chinese metaphorical sentences only concern six prototype processes and seven model processes. Secondly, the same source processes in English metaphorical sentences seem to be able to map on more target domain processes than in Chinese. Behavioural processes, for example, can be mapped on all the other seven processes in English, but they can only be mapped on six other processes in Chinese. Whereas English existential processes can serve as the source domain of seven processes, Chinese existential processes can just work as the prototype for two processes. Thirdly, six processes in English can be used metaphorically to express the meaning of a complex sentence; only one process in Chinese can be thus used. Finally, there seem to be more metaphorical mappings in English than in Chinese. While English metaphorical mappings total up to 38, Chinese metaphorical mappings only number 24 though neither of them amounts to the theoretically possible 64.

One thing to be pointed out is that this study is not comprehensive enough to cover all kinds of metaphorical mappings in English and Chinese. There might be other incongruent transferences that the author has not found. What matters here is that metaphorical sentences are used incongruently by mapping one or one kind of process onto another, so they involve noncorresponding relationship between the verb on the one hand, and the Subject, and/or the Object/ Complement on the other.

4.6 Relationship Between Metaphorical Sentences and Nonmetaphorical Sentences

In concluding the chapter, the author deems it necessary to make a brief summary of the relationship between metaphorical sentences and nonmetaphorical sentences.

As shown by the examples in these two chapters, metaphorical sentences and nonmetaphorical sentences are closely related in meaning and structure. Semantically, metaphorical sentences and their corresponding nonmetaphorical sentences are supposed to be the same. The relationship between them is a logical one, that is, a synonymous one. Therefore, metaphorical sentences are supposed to express the meaning of nonmetaphorical sentences in the last two chapters. However, one cannot reasonably expect a metaphorical sentence and a nonmetaphorical sentence to be totally synonymous. "The selection of metaphor is itself a meaningful choice, and the particular metaphor selected adds further semantic features." (Halliday, 1994: 342) The congruent and the incongruent versions, in Halliday's term, are only "systematically related in meaning, and therefore synonymous in certain respects". In the following example, (b) is the incongruent form and (c) is the congruent form. They are understood as synonymous to some extent. Actually, they are different. Firstly, the processes used are different. One is in a behavioural process while the other is in a sensuous process. Secondly, the information structure is different. The theme is *a sudden impulse* in (b), but it is *I* in (c). Finally, (c) is a stative statement while (b) is a dynamic description. All the factors above show that the two sentences are somewhat different in meaning.

(79) (b) A sudden impulse *seized* me to visit Thrushcross.
(c) I suddenly wanted to visit Thrushcross.

Structurally, metaphorical sentences and their corresponding nonmetaphorical sentences are also supposed to be the same. The relationship between them is an embryological one. So, in the last two chapters, the author deems them to be of the same sentence pattern. This is true, indeed, because metaphorical sentences are usually modeled on nonmetaphorical sentences in structure. In the following example, (a) is a nonmetaphorical sentence and (b) is a metaphorical sentence since (b) does not have the normal Behaver or the normal Patient that the process usually requires. (b) is modeled on (a) in structure.

(80) (a) Tom gave Mary a book.
(b) The film *gave* us much pleasure.

However, generally speaking, metaphorical sentences and their corresponding nonmetaphorical sentences cannot be the same both in structure and in meaning. If a metaphorical sentence and a nonmetaphorical sentence are the same in structure, they are usually different in meaning, as is shown in (80). On the contrary, if a metaphorical sentence and a nonmetaphorical sentence are the same (to some extent) in meaning, they are usually different in structure, which has been shown by (79). But of course there are exceptions. When a metaphorical sentence and a corresponding nonmetaphorical sentence are both embodied in SVC sentence pattern, they are fundamentally the same both in structure and in meaning. For example:

(81) (b) The earth is thirsty.
(c) The earth is dry.

In this example, (b) is metaphorical and (c) is nonmetaphorical. But they are of the same structure, namely, the same SVC pattern. In other words, the metaphorical sentence and the nonmetaphorical sentence are the same both in meaning and in structure. However, this kind of example seems to be few in English and Chinese. Sometimes even though the sentence patterns are the same, the structure may be analyzed differently. For instance:

(82) (b) He is an eagle.
(c) He is brave.

In this example, the metaphorical sentence and the nonmetaphorical sentence are both expressed in SVC pattern. But we may still argue that the two sentences are different in structure because the Complement is realized by a noun phrase in (b) and by an adjective phrase in (c).

Moreover, some metaphorical sentences are difficult to recognize. They are often regarded as nonmetaphorical by common people, because they are used too frequently. However, logical analysis will show clearly that they are still metaphorical sentences. For example:

(83) The tourist season *extends* from May till October.
(84) 我们一定要*根除*这种不良状况。

These two sentences are so common in English and Chinese that they are seldom considered as metaphorical by native speakers. However, they are really metaphorical if they are analyzed logically. The material verb process *extend* usually requires an extendable physical entity such as a road or a river represented by the Subject. But sentence (83) does not satisfy this requirement and has a Subject denoting an abstract entity. Similarly, the verb *根除* should have an Object denoting plants, but sentence (84) does not meet the requirement. Therefore, the two sentences are in fact metaphorical sentences. One is represented by the Subject-verb transitivity system, the other is represented by the verb-Object transitivity system.

Chapter Five

Translation of English Metaphorical Sentences into Chinese

Although metaphorical sentences in English and Chinese are generated via the same mechanisms of personification, animalization, plantification, hypostatization and alienation, and represented by the same transitivity systems between Subject-verb relationships, verb-Object relationships, and Subject-verb-Object/Complement relationships, there are still some differences between English metaphorical sentences and Chinese metaphorical sentences. Without accurate statistics to support this point of view, the author thinks it reasonable to illustrate the differences by means of E-C translation.

As discussed above, there do not seem to be as many metaphorical sentences in Chinese as in English. In other words, there seem to be more metaphorical sentences in English than in Chinese.

Therefore, this chapter will discuss how English metaphorical sentences are expressed in Chinese or how they are translated into Chinese.

If it happens that a Chinese verb can be used metaphorically to express the meaning of other processes as a corresponding English verb, English metaphorical sentences can be translated into Chinese metaphorical sentences directly. For example:

(1) Rome *witness*ed many great historic events.
罗马城*目睹*过许多伟大的历史性事件。

(2) Time *permitting*, I will go to see you.
如果时间*允许*的话，我一定去看你。

(3) The work *met with* failure.
这项工作*遇到*失败。

(4) He *made* no answer to the question.
对这个问题，他不*作*回答。

(5) The thick carpet *killed* the sound of my footsteps.
厚地毯*湮灭了*脚步的声音。

(6) Peace *brings* prosperity.
和平可以*带来*繁荣。

(7) Pure gold *fears* not the fire.
真金不*怕*火炼。

(8) Let's *lay* the problem *aside*.
这个问题咱们先*搁一搁*。

(9) He *broke* two national records that evening.
那天晚上，他*打破了*两项全国记录。

(10) A hearty welcome *awaits* you.
热情的欢迎*等待*着你。

(11) Their national spirit *awoke*.
他们的民族精神*觉醒*了。

In these examples, English metaphorical sentences are translated directly into Chinese metaphorical sentences. However, while all the English metaphorical sentences sound natural and appropriate, some of the Chinese metaphorical sentences seem to be odd and unnatural. They will sound more natural if they are translated into nonmetaphorical sentences. (1) and (5) may be translated as the following:

在罗马城发生过许多伟大的历史性事件。
我走在厚厚的地毯上，一点脚步声也没有。

Things are remarkably like this when the metaphorical sentences involve an incongruent relationship of Subject-verb or Subject-verb-Object/Complement transitivity systems. This is because, as mentioned above, there is a clearcut distinction between animate verbs and inanimate verbs in Chinese. Animate verbs are seldom used together with inanimate Subjects. In Chinese only animate beings can initiate conscious behaviours and actions. Therefore, the Senser, the Behaver, the Thinker and the Sayer are almost always human beings. Inanimate objects do not have conscious behaviours or actions. Generally, they cannot be used with animate verbs. However, some nouns denoting abstract entities could be used with animate verbs in Chinese through the mechanism of personification. No wonder some writers like to use animate verbs with inanimate Subjects in Chinese. This is probably due to the influence of some foreign languages. One example is Lu Xun. Such sentences can be found in his works. For example:

(12) 这寂寞又一天一天*长大*起来，如大毒蛇，缠住了我的灵魂。（《呐喊》自序）
(13) 四十多个青年的血，*洋溢*在我的周围，使我艰于呼吸视

听，哪里还能有什么言语？（《纪念刘和珍君》）

(14) 这并非为了别的，只因为两年以来，悲愤总时时来*袭击*我的心，至今没有停止。（《为了忘却的纪念》）

But animate verbs and inanimate verbs are not distinguished so clearly in English. Many animate verbs can be used freely with inanimate Subjects. These verbs include *do*, *see*, *have*, *get*, *send*, *invite*, *take*, *find*, *rise*, *grow*, *know*, *drive*, etc. Therefore, most English metaphorical sentences cannot be translated into Chinese metaphorical sentences directly. They are usually translated into nonmetaphorical sentences or more congruent sentences. Hence, this chapter will center on the translation of English metaphorical sentences into Chinese nonmetaphorical sentences. The strategies are discussed as follows.

5.1 Translating English Metaphorical Sentences into Chinese Animate Sentences

If English metaphorical sentences involve an incongruent relationship of Subject-verb or Subject-verb-Object/Complement transitivity systems, they are usually used to express congruently animate sentences. Therefore, it is easy and convenient to translate them into Chinese animate sentences.

5.1.1 Translating English Metaphorical Sentences Directly into Chinese Animate Sentences

Some English metaphorical sentences can be translated directly into Chinese animate sentences. The first step is to find the right animate Subject of the sentence. Then make some changes in the arrangement of other elements in the sentence. For example:

(15) An idea suddenly *occurred* to me.
我突然想到了一个主意。

(16) That night sleep *eluded* me.
那天晚上，我没有睡好。

(17) The plan *strikes* me as ridiculous.
我觉得那项计划很荒唐。

(18) Despair *seized* him (at the thought of her setting out alone to renew the weary quest for work).
(一想到她孤零零地重新踏上寻找工作的艰辛历程，) 他就觉得万念俱灰。

(19) A chill of horror suddenly *swept over* him.
他突然感到不寒而栗。

(20) Rarely did his sense of humour *desert* the noble man.
这位高尚的人很少失去幽默感。

(21) All my courage *deserted* me.
我完全丧失了勇气。

(22) Sleep didn't *visit* Rainsford (although the silence of a dead world was on the jungle).
(尽管丛林里是死一般的寂静) 雷恩斯福德还是不能入睡。

(23) Hope *persisted* in Marshall (because the only alternative was a military solution).
马歇尔没有放弃希望（不然的话就得军事解决）。

(24) My admiration for him *grew* more.
我对他越发敬佩。

(25) Reproach *spared* him not, even when in his grave.

他即使在死后也不能免于遭受人们的非难。

(26) A smile *rested* on her lips.
她嘴角上露出了微笑。

(27) My ears *are singing*.
我有些耳鸣。

(28) A suspicion *sprang up* in his mind.
他脑中产生了一些怀疑。

(29) Pity *stirred* in her heart.
她心中产生了怜悯的感情。

(30) Suddenly a happy thought *struck* her.
她突然有了一个很妙的想法。

(31) Age *was telling* on him.
他慢慢感到衰老了。

(32) Her mind *travelled* over recent events.
她想到了最近发生的许多事情。

(33) His thought *wandered back* to his college days.
他回想起大学的那些日子。

(34) American education *owes* a great debt to Thomas Jefferson.
托马斯·杰弗逊对美国的教育事业做出了巨大的贡献。

(35) Fury *took* possession of him.
他一下子怒不可遏。

(36) Her face always *wore* a cheerful smile.
她脸上老带着愉快的笑容。

In the examples above, most English metaphorical sentences are represented by Subject-verb transitivity systems except the last two, which are represented by Subject-verb-Object transitivity systems. Though all the original sentences have inanimate Subjects, they are translated into animate sentences in Chinese.

5.1.2 Translating English Metaphorical Sentences into Chinese Animate Sentences by Changing the Inanimate Subjects into Adverbials

When English metaphorical sentences are translated into Chinese animate sentences, the original Subjects may be translated into adverbials.

If the Subject of the English metaphorical sentence is realized by a noun phrase of time, the Subject is sometimes translated into an adverbial of time. For instance:

(37) Dawn *met* him well along the road.
东方破晓的时候，他早已上路。

(38) October, 1979 *found* me studying in England.
1979 年 10 月份的时候，我在英国学习。

(39) Ten days would *disband* his corps and *leave* him 1400 men.
十天以后，他的军队就土崩瓦解，他也就剩下 1400 名士兵了。

(40) The postwar years in Germany saw honours heaped upon the great scientist.
在德国战后的岁月里，这位伟大的科学家得到了种种荣誉。

In all these examples, the inanimate Subjects of time in the English metaphorical sentences are translated into adverbials of time in Chinese. The predicates are translated into animate sentences.

Sometimes, the inanimate Subjects denoting abstract entities, acts and facts can also be translated into Chinese adverbials of other kinds. Look at the following examples:

(41) Business *took* him to the town.
他因事进城去了。

(42) A just regard to the constitution and to the duty of my office *forbids* a compliance with your request.
为了遵守宪法，为了履行我的职责，我不能同意你的请求。

(43) Losing his fortune *drove* him mad.
他由于失去财产而发疯。

In the examples above, the predicate of each English metaphorical sentence is translated into an animate sentence while the inanimate Subject is translated into an adverbial.

5.2 Translating English Metaphorical Sentences into Chinese Complex Sentences

As discussed in the last two chapters, many English process types can be used metaphorically to express the meaning of complex sentences. Therefore, when these metaphorical sentences are translated into nonmetaphorical sentences in Chinese, they are usually translated into complex sentences. While the predicates are translated into animate sentences, the original inanimate Subjects are translated into adverbial clauses. For example:

(44) The sight of the river *reminds* me of my hometown.
一看到这条河，我便想起了我的故乡。

(45) The loss of Lee *was* a severe shock to the Americans.
李将军被俘后，美国朝野上下大为震惊。

(46) Our violent attack *sent* the enemy troops flying in all

directions.

在我方的猛烈攻击下，敌军士兵向四面八方逃窜。

(47) The rain *prevented* me from coming.

因下雨，我没能来。

(48) My duty *forbids* me to fly from danger.

职责所在，我不能临阵脱逃。

(49) Shortness of time *has required* his omission of some states.

由于时间不够，他不能访问某些国家了。

(50) The thought of seeing her son very soon *filled* her heart with great happiness.

想到不久就要看到她的儿子，她心中感到十分快乐。

(51) Only the thought of his mother *gave* him the strength to go on doing it.

只是由于想起了他的母亲，他才鼓起了勇气继续干下去。

(52) The least alarm of their movement would *bring* the enemy upon them and *produce* a terrible scene of confusion and carnage at the place of embarkation.

只要他们的行动有一丝一毫惊动敌人，敌人就会立即进攻，在登陆地点大肆进行屠杀，造成一片可怕的混乱局面。

(53) Careful comparison of them will *show* you the difference.

只要仔细比较一下，你就会发现它们的差异。

(54) A little time and perseverance will *give* us some favourable opportunity of recovering our loss.

只要假以时日，只要我们坚持不懈，我们终究会找到某种有利的时机收复失地。

In the examples above, English metaphorical sentences are translated into complex sentences in Chinese. The inanimate Subjects are all translated into adverbial clauses. Sentences (44) – (45) involve adverbial clauses of time, (46) – (51) those of reason and (52) – (54) those of condition.

5.3 Translating English Metaphorical Sentences into Chinese Compound Sentences

If English metaphorical sentences can be translated into Chinese complex sentences, they can be translated into compound sentences in Chinese since complex sentences and compound sentences usually have a relation of "systematic correspondence" (Quirk, et al, 1985: 57). The difference is that the logical relationship between the clauses is overt in a complex sentence but covert in a compound sentence. Consider the following examples:

(55) A few steps along the corridor *brought* me to a large hall.
我沿着走廊走了几步，就到了一个华丽的大厅。

(56) Fortunately the dense fog *had prevented* the enemy from discovering that the lines were unoccupied.
幸而大雾沉沉，敌人并没有发现（美军）前线无人防守。

(57) His words *sent* a quiver through my body.
我听了他的话，不禁打了个寒战。

(58) His adventurous exploits soon *won* him notoriety.
他作战英勇，屡建战功，很快就名声远扬。

(59) An 80-minute drive *took* us to the Ming Tombs' Reservoir.
汽车开了 80 分钟，我们来到十三陵水库。

(60) Absence and distance *make* the overseas Chinese heart increasingly fond of Beijing.

海外华人远离故土，千里迢迢地旅居异乡，自然越来越怀念北京。

In these examples, English metaphorical sentences are translated into Chinese compound sentences. While the predicates are translated into animate clauses, the Subjects are translated into a coordinate clause. Though the relationship between the coordinate clauses in each Chinese sentence is not overt, it can be made clear without effort. While sentences (55) and (59) have temporal relationships, all the other sentences involve causal relationships.

These three sections have presented a study on different methods of translating English metaphorical sentences into Chinese nonmetaphorical sentences. Though the English metaphorical sentences are all inanimate sentences, the Chinese translations all involve animate Subjects. In the complex sentences, usually the superordinate clauses are animate. In the compound sentences, either coordinate clause may be animate.

When an English metaphorical sentence is translated into an animate sentence in Chinese, it must involve a human participant or an implied human participant. Otherwise, the English metaphorical sentence cannot be translated into an animate sentence in Chinese. (See 5.6)

Sometimes, however, even when the English metaphorical sentence involves a human participant or an implied human participant, it cannot be translated into an animate sentence in Chinese, either. (Also refer to 5.6)

5.4 Translating English Metaphorical Sentences into Chinese Subjectless Sentences

Sometimes, English metaphorical sentences can be translated into Chinese subjectless sentences if it is difficult to find a suitable subject. For instance:

(61) The perspective in which this journey must be placed *goes back* to Bandung.
要正确了解此行的意义，必须追溯到万隆会议。

(62) The heavy rain *visited* the city.
这个城市刚下过一场大雨。

(63) A bold stroke would *free* the land from rapine devastation and brutal outrage.
只要打一个漂亮仗，就能使国土免遭掠夺破坏和野蛮的蹂躏。

(64) The mastery of a language *requires* painstaking effort.
要学好一种外语，必须下苦工夫。

5.5 Translating English Metaphorical Sentences into Chinese Indefinite Subject Sentences

English metaphorical sentences can also be translated into Chinese indefinite subject sentences. For example:

(65) Dusk *found* the little girl crying in the street.

黄昏时分，人们发现这个小女孩在街上哭。

(66) The 19th century *saw* experiments to make concrete stronger by reinforcing it with iron bars.
19 世纪，人们做过一些实验，用钢筋加固混凝土。

(67) Her falling ill would *spoil* everything.
如果她生病了，一切就会变糟。

5.6 Translating English Metaphorical Sentences into Chinese Inanimate Sentences

When an English metaphorical sentence does not involve a human participant or an implied human participant, it is often translated into an inanimate sentence in Chinese. Necessary changes should be made. For example:

(68) Britain *saw* the first jet airplane in 1952.
第一架喷气式飞机于 1952 年在英国诞生。

(69) The plane *responds* well to the controls.
这架飞机控制系统很灵。

(70) The engine *suffered* severely as a result.
结果，发动机受到严重损害。

(71) In 1919 the May 4th Movement *swept* the country.
1919 年，五四运动席卷全国。

(72) Time *works* many changes.
时间会带来许多变化。

(73) Spring *wakes* all nature.
春天使大自然觉醒。

(74) The arrest of the flood-waters *saved* many homes.

洪水拦住之后，许多家庭得救了。

(75) A sudden shower *killed* the wind.
突如其来的阵雨，使大风停息下来。

(76) The application of special additional device *permits* the car to run faster than before.
只要使用一种专用的附加装置，这辆汽车就可以跑得更快。

(77) There *was* no reduction in the price.
价格没有降低。

(78) A hush *fell upon* the assembly.
会场一片寂静。

(79) The world *has witnessed* different roads to modernization.
世界上已经有不同的现代化道路。

Note that sentences (74) and (76) are translated into complex sentences, in which the superordinate clauses have inanimate Subjects. (78) and (79) are translated into existential sentences, of which the Subjects are inanimate locations.

Sometimes, however, even when the English metaphorical sentence involves a human participant or an implied human participant, it can be translated into an inanimate sentence in Chinese. For example:

(80) The news completely *upset* them.
这消息使他们很难受。

(81) Their drive *moved* us deeply.
他们的干劲使我们深受感动。

(82) Liberation *found* my hometown with few hospitals.
解放时，我的故乡医院很少。

(83) His addition *completed* the list.

把他添上以后，名单就完备了。

(84) Darkness would *make* him more appreciative of sight; silence would *teach* him the joys of sound.
黑暗使人更加珍惜光明；寂静教人体会到声音的欢乐。

(85) Daylight will *reveal* the disposition of their troops.
天亮之后，他们军队的部署就会显露出来。

(86) These words *stirred* her deeply.
这些话使她深受触动。

(87) The expenses nearly *swallowed up* all his earnings.
这些开支几乎把他挣的钱全部耗费掉了。

(88) Hot baths *do* me much good.
热水浴对我大有好处。

(89) A nail *caught* her dress.
一枚钉子挂住了她的衣裳。

(90) The title of the book *invites* the reader's interest.
书的名称引起了读者的兴趣。

(91) His hint *escaped* me.
他的暗示没有引起我的注意。

(92) There *is* a reference to Tom in my book.
我的书中提到汤姆。

In these examples, though English metaphorical sentences each involve a human participant or an implied human participant, they are translated into Chinese inanimate sentences. Of course, some of them can be translated into animate sentences. (91) and (92), for example, can be translated as:

我没有注意到他的暗示。
我在书中提到汤姆。

However, the inanimate sentences sound more natural in

Chinese.

Up to now, the English metaphorical sentences provided in the preceding sections were all represented by Subject-verb or Subject-verb-Object/Complement transitivity systems. Those that are represented by verb-Object transitivity systems will be discussed in the following.

Compared with the other two kinds of metaphorical sentences, those that are represented by verb-Object transitivity systems can be translated into Chinese more easily. They are usually translated into Chinese with the same Subjects, making necessary adjustment in the predicates. For instance:

(93) She *is doing* her knitting.
她在打毛衣。

(94) He *took* no notice of my complaints.
他没有注意到我的不满。

(95) I *have* an esteem for him.
我尊敬他。

(96) He *embraced* my offer.
他欣然接受了我的建议。

(97) They *put* an advertisement in the newspaper.
他们在报纸上登了一则广告。

(98) We would never *pick* a fight with them.
我们决不向他们挑衅。

(99) I have *picked up* a great deal of information.
我已经搜集到很多资料。

(100) The prisoners *received* harsh and unfair treatment.
俘虏们受到粗暴的不公平的对待。

(101) Then she *turned* her attention to another problem.
这时，她把注意力转向了另一个问题。

(102) They *weighed* the matter seriously.
他们认真地考虑了这件事。

However, sometimes the Subject of an English metaphorical sentence has to be changed to suit the Chinese expression. Look at the following two examples:

(103) Everybody *sees* imperialism growing weaker.
帝国主义日趋衰落。

(104) He *had* justice on his side.
正义在他的一边。

5.7 Summary

This chapter has discussed how to translate English metaphorical sentences into Chinese. Altogether, six methods or strategies are proposed. The six strategies are translating English metaphorical sentences into Chinese animate sentences, complex sentences, compound sentences, subjectless sentences, indefinite subject sentences and inanimate sentences. However, they are far from being exhaustive. In practice, one must translate English metaphorical sentences according to the meaning and the context of the original sentence. The translated version should be both equivalent to the original sentence in meaning and appropriate in Chinese expression.

Chapter Six

Conclusion

This book has presented a contrastive study of metaphorical sentences in English and Chinese. Of the preceding five chapters, Chapter One is the introduction. Chapter Two discusses the generative mechanisms of metaphorical sentences in English and Chinese. Chapter Three and Chapter Four are about the representation of metaphorical sentences in the two languages. Chapter Five talks about the translation of English metaphorical sentences into Chinese. This chapter will summarize the whole book, draw some tentative conclusions and outline the areas worthy of my future study on and around this topic.

6.1 Summary

As stated in the introduction, the primary objective of the present study is to make more comprehensive and more explicative Zhang Jin's theory of the generation of sentence patterns to better explain the relationship between sentences. This study is an extension and elaboration of his theory. Specifically, the current research is designed to make a tentative study on metaphorical sentences in English and Chinese. It focuses on the generation and the representation of metaphorical sentences in the two languages.

On the basis of the previous studies on metaphor, the author suggests that metaphorization be one of the generative mechanisms of sentences. Thus the whole structure of Zhang Jin's theory includes the generation of the basic sentence patterns directly from reality and the other four generative mechanisms of combination, substitution, transformation and metaphorization from the basic sentence patterns. The addition of the metaphorical mechanism makes Zhang Jin's theory more comprehensive and more explicative.

If the author is right in assuming that metaphorization is a mechanism of generating sentences, sentences can be divided into two groups: metaphorical sentences and nonmetaphorical sentences. Metaphorical sentences are generated by metaphorical mechanisms. Nonmetaphorical sentences are those directly modeled upon the relation of the entities in reality.

A metaphorical sentence is defined in this book **as a sentence in which the relationships between the verb on the one hand and the**

Subject, and/or the Object/Complement on the other are incongruent with or uncorresponding to reality. Therefore, incongruent relationships in metaphorical sentences may occur between the predicate verb and the Subject, and the predicate verb and the Object, and also the Subject, the predicate verb and the Object/Complement.

The approach adopted in this book is genuinely cognition-oriented. Though theories of different schools are mentioned, they all offer a dialectic view on language which allows interaction between language, reality and cognition.

In the frontier of cognitive linguistics, metaphor is explained with more explanatory power. According to Lakoff and Johnson (1980), metaphor is a cross-domain mapping in the conceptual system. It is generated by mapping a source domain concept onto a target domain concept on the basis of resemblance in the broad sense. Resemblance includes not only physical resemblance, sensational resemblance, but also mental resemblance, imaginary resemblance or creative resemblance. It also includes contiguity and analogy. When one thing or one kind of thing is mapped onto another conceptually, it can be expressed linguistically instead of the other. Conceptual metaphors lead to linguistic metaphors.

Since the development of human cognition is, as a rule, from tangible concrete entities to intangible and abstract entities and then to nonentities, people are inclined to model abstract things on concrete things. They understand abstract things in terms of concrete things through their understandings of human beings, animals, plants and inanimate objects. When they express other things in terms of the concrete things mentioned, they make a metaphorical sentence. In other words, metaphorical sentences are created by means of personification, animalization, plantification, hypostatization and alienation.

However, when man gets to know the world, he does it not merely by impressing the names of the separate things on his mind, but by realizing an individual thing's features, behaviour, action and its relation with other things. All these can be typically expressed in a transitivity system of verb processes. Therefore, when one thing is modeled on another, it also adopts the features, the behaviour and the action of another. When one process is used to express the meaning of another process, there emerges a metaphorical sentence. Metaphorical sentences usually involve incongruent relationships between the verb and the Subject, or the verb and the Object, or the verb and the Subject on the one hand and the Object/ Complement on the other. In other words, metaphorical sentences are represented by Subject-verb transitivity systems, verb-Object transitivity systems, and Subject-verb-Object/Complement transitivity systems.

Although metaphorical sentences in English and Chinese are generated via the same mechanisms of personification, animalization, plantification, hypostatization and alienation, and represented by the same transitivity systems between Subject-verb relationships, verb-Object relationships, and Subject-verb-Object/Complement relationships, there are still some differences between English metaphorical sentences and Chinese metaphorical sentences. Without accurate statistics to support this point of view, the author thinks it reasonable to make an illustration of the differences by means of E-C translation.

In general, the empirical interlingual contrastive studies presented in this book support the assumption that metaphorization is one of the generative mechanisms of sentences.

6.2 Conclusions

It is hoped that the preceding discussions can lay a sound basis for the following tentative conclusions:

1) Metaphorization is one of the generative mechanisms of sentences since many sentences in English and Chinese are generated via metaphorization.
2) Metaphorical sentences are generated through personification, animalization, plantification, hypostatization and alienation.
3) Metaphorical sentences are represented by the incongruent relationships of Subject-verb, verb-Object and Subject-verb-Object/Complement transitivity systems.
4) There seem to be more kinds of metaphorical sentences in English than in Chinese.
5) Metaphorical mappings are not arbitrary, but grounded in our bodily experience and daily knowledge. The degree of similarity between English and Chinese is very illustrative.
6) Metaphorical mappings are also culture specific. Different cultural models in different languages may dictate different choices of linguistic realizations. The degree of difference between English and Chinese is very explanatory.

These findings suggest that the present study has the following implications:

1) The combination of the research of metaphor with the research of grammar is complementary to the research of the two domains.

2) Contrastive research helps understand better some of the different features of English and Chinese.
3) The interlingual study of metaphorical sentences is helpful to the contrastive study between the two languages. It enables us to go deeper into the thinking modes and habits of different peoples, rather than merely comparing the formal resemblances or differences.
4) The present work is also of great help to language teaching, especially foreign language teaching. It is particularly useful to Chinese learners of English and English learners of Chinese.
5) This study is helpful, too, to the practice of translation between English and Chinese.

6.3 Suggested Areas for Future Study

Though some fundamental issues of metaphorical sentences have been analyzed and elaborated in this book, the author is quite conscious that the present study is not comprehensive and is still very preliminary. There are still a number of related topics that remain untreated and there are also some problems that remain unsolved. The following may be some of the possible topics:

1) The evidence may not be strong enough because only two languages are discussed. Other languages, such as French, German, Japanese and Russian, should be investigated in future. Moreover, the data is only provided from modern English and Chinese. If some examples can be offered from classical works, the results will be more convincing. Finally, the range of the data

is not wide enough to explain all kinds of metaphorical sentences and their mappings. More comprehensive investigation should be done in future.

2) The present work is just an empirical qualitative study. Quantitative study should be adopted as well in future.
3) Though the book has found some similarities and differences between English and Chinese metaphorical sentences, it fails to provide an adequate explanation of them for lack of time and space.
4) The application of metaphorical sentences in the study of other linguistic fields is not taken up in the present study for lack of time and space. This will be dealt with in future studies.

Bibliography

Alexander, L. G. Longman English Grammar. New York: Longman, 1988.

Aronoff, M. & J. Rees-Miller. The Handbook of Linguistics. Oxford: Blackwell, 2001.

Austin, J. L. How to Do Things with Words. Oxford: Oxford University Press, 1962.

Baltin, M. & C. Collins. The Handbook of Contemporary Syntactic Theory. Oxford: Blackwell, 2000.

Beaugrande. R. Linguistic Theory: The Discourse of Fundamental Works. London: Longman, 1991.

Biber, D. et al. Longman Grammar of Spoken and Written English. London: Longman, 1999.

Bloomfield, L. Language. Chicago: The University of Chicago Press, 1933.

Bloor, T. & M. Bloor. The Functional Analysis of English: A Hallidayan Approach. London: Edward Arnold, 1995.

Bussmann, H. Routledge Dictionary of Language and Linguistics. London: Routledge, 1996.

Cameron, L. & G. Low. ed. Researching and Applying Metaphor. Cambridge: Cambridge University Press, 1999.

Carroll, D. W. Psychology of Language (3rd edition). Monterey CA: Brooks/Cole Publishing Company, 1999.

Chomsky, N. Syntactic Structures. The Hague: Mouton, 1957.

Chomsky, N. Aspects of the Theory of Syntax. Cambridge: The MIT Press, 1965.

Comrie, B. Language Universals and Linguistic Typology. Chicago: University of Chicago Press, 1989.

Croft, W. Typology and Universals. Cambridge: Cambridge University Press, 1990.

Culicover, P. W. Syntax (2nd edition). New York and London: Academic Press Inc., 1982.

Dobrzyska,T. "Translating Metaphor: Problems of Meaning". Journal of Pragmatics 24(1995), 595-604.

Emanation, M. "Congruence by Degree: On the Relation between Metaphor and Cultural Models". In Metaphor in Cognitive Linguistics. Ed. Gibbs, R.W. Jr. & G. J. Steen. Amsterdam: John Benjamins Publishing Company, 1999, 205-218.

Fan, Wenfang. A Systemic-Functional Approach to Grammatical Metaphor. Beijing: Foreign Language Teaching and Research Press, 2001.

Feng, Cuihua. English Rhetorical Options—A Handbook of English Rhetorical Devices. Beijing: Foreign Language Teaching and Research Press, 1995.

Foley, W. A. Anthropological Linguistics: An Introduction. Oxford: Blackwell, 1997.

Gee, J. P. An Introduction to Discourse Analysis: Theory and Method. London: Routledge, 1999.

Gibbs, R.W. Jr. & G. J. Steen. ed. Metaphor in Cognitive Linguistics. Amsterdam: John Benjamins Publishing Company, 1999.

Grady, J. "A Typology of Motivation for Conceptual Metaphor: Correlation vs. Resemblance". In Metaphor in Cognitive Linguistics. Ed. Gibbs, R.W. Jr. & G. J. Steen. Amsterdam: John Benjamins Publishing Company, 1999, 79-100.

Green, G. M. Pragmatics and Natural Language Understanding. New Jersey: Lawrence Inc., 1996.

Grice, P. Studies in the Way of Words. Cambridge: Harvard University Press, 1989.

Halliday, M. A. K. Language as Social Semiotic: The Social Interpretation of Language and Meaning. London: Edward and Arnold, 1978.

Halliday, M. A. K. An Introduction to Functional Grammar (2nd edition). London: Edward and Arnold, 1994.

Halliday, M. A. K. and R. Hasan. Cohesion in English. London: Longman, 1976.

Hirga, M. K. "Diagrams and Metaphors: Iconic Aspects in Language". Journal of Pragmatics 22 (1994), 5-21.

Hopper, P. J. & E. C. Traugott. Grammaticalization. Cambridge: Cambridge University Press, 1993.

Hornby, A. S. Oxford Advanced Learner's Dictionary of Current English (4th edition). Oxford: Oxford University Press, 1974.

Itkonen, E. "Iconicity, Analogy, and Universal Grammar". Journal of Pragmatics 22(1994), 37-53.

Jespersen, O. The Philosophy of Grammar. London: Allen and Unwin, 1924.

Kitty, E. F. Metaphor: Its Cognitive Force and Linguistic Structure. Oxford: Clarendon Press, 1987.

Kuteva, T. "Iconicity and Auxiliation". Journal of Pragmatics 22(1994), 71-81.

Kövecses, Z. "Metaphor: Does It Constitute or Reflect Cultural Models?" In Metaphor in Cognitive Linguistics. Ed. Gibbs, R.W. Jr. & G. J. Steen. Amsterdam: John Benjamins Publishing Company, 1999, 167-188.

Lakoff, G. & M. Johnson. Metaphors We Live By. Chicago: The University of Chicago Press, 1980.

Lakoff, G. Women, Fire, and Dangerous Things: What Categories Reveal about the Mind. Chicago: The University of Chicago Press, 1987.

Langacker, R. W. "An Introduction to Cognitive Grammar". Cognitive Science 10(1986), 1-40.

Langacker, R. W. Foundations of Cognitive Grammar (Vol. I). Stanford: Stanford University Press, 1987.

Lappin, S. The Handbook of Contemporary Semantic Theory. Oxford: Blackwell, 1997.

Leech, G. Style in Fiction: A Linguistic Introduction to English Fictional Prose. London: Longman, 1981.

Leech, G. et al. English Grammar for Today. London: The Macmillan Press, 1982.

Leech, G. Principles of Pragmatics. New York: Longman, 1983.

Lehmann, W. Historical Linguistics: An Introduction. London: Routledge, 1992.

Levinson, S. C. Pragmatics. Cambridge: Cambridge University Press, 1983.

Lyons, J. Linguistic Semantics: An Introduction. Cambridge:

Cambridge University Press, 1995.

Mahon, J. E. "Getting Your Source Right: What Aristotle didn't Say". In Researching and Applying Metaphor. Ed. Cameron, L. & G. Low. Cambridge: Cambridge University Press, 1999, 69-80.

Mey, J. Pragmatics: An Introduction (2nd edition). Oxford: Blackwell, 1993.

Niu, Baoyi. Belief and Doubt: Epistemology of Tag Question. Ph.D Dissertation. Kaifeng: Henan University, 2001.

Packard, J. L. The Morphology of Chinese: A Linguistic and Cognitive Approach. Cambridge: Cambridge University Press, 2000.

Palmer, F. R. Grammar. London: Penguin, 1971.

Ponterotto, D. "Metaphors We Can Learn By". English Teaching Forum 3(1994), 2-7.

Peccei, J. S. Pragmatics. London: Routledge, 1999.

Quirk, R. et al. A Grammar of Contemporary English. London: Longman, 1972.

Quirk, R. et al. A Comprehensive Grammar of the English Language. London: Longman, 1985.

Radwańska-Williams, J. "The Problem of Iconicity". Journal of Pragmatics 22(1994), 23-36.

Richards, J. C. et al. Longman Dictionary of Language Teaching & Applied Linguistics. London: Longman, 1992.

Roberts, W. H. & G. Turgeon. About Language: A Reader for Writers (5th edition). Beijing: Foreign Language Teaching and Research Press, 2000.

Robins, R. H. A Short History of Linguistics. London: Longman, 1997.

Saeed, J. I. Semantics. Oxford: Blackwell, 1997.

Samovar, L. A. et al. Communication Between Cultures (3rd edition). Beijing: Foreign Language Teaching and Research Press, 2000.

Sapir, E. Language: An Introduction to the Study of Speech. New York: Harcourt Brace Jovanovich Inc., 1921.

Saussure, de F. Course in General Linguistics. Trans. Baskin. W. New York: Philosophical Library Inc., 1959.

Schiffrin, D. Discourse Marker. Cambridge: Cambridge University Press, 1987.

Searle, J. R. Speech Acts: An Essay in the Philosophy of Language. Cambridge: Cambridge University Press, 1969.

Searle, J. R. Expression and Meaning: Studies in the Theory of Speech Acts. Cambridge: Cambridge University Press, 1979.

Slade, C. Form and Style: Research Papers, Reports and Theses (10th edition). Beijing: Foreign Language Teaching and Research Press, 2000.

Smith, N. Chomsky: Ideas and Ideals. Cambridge: Cambridge University Press, 1999.

Smith, N. & D. Wilson. Modern Linguistics: The Results of Chomskyan Revolution. London: Penguin, 1979.

Sperber, D. & D. Wilson. Relevance: Communication and Cognition (2nd edition). Oxford: Blackwell, 1995.

Steen, G. "Metaphor and Discourse: Toward a Linguistic Checklist for Metaphor Analysis". In Researching and Applying Metaphor. Ed. Cameron, L. & G. Low. Cambridge: Cambridge University Press, 1999, 81-104.

Steen, G. "From Linguistic to Conceptual Metaphor in Five Steps". In Metaphor in Cognitive Linguistics. Ed. Gibbs, R.W. Jr. & G. J. Steen. Amsterdam: John Benjamins Publishing Company, 1999, 57-78.

Sweetser, E. From Etymology to Pragmatics: Metaphorical and Cultural Aspects of Semantic Structure. Cambridge: Cambridge University Press, 1990.

Sweetser, E. "Metaphor, Mythology, and Everyday Language". Journal of Pragmatics 24 (1995), 585-593.

Taylor, J. R. Linguistic Categorization: Prototypes in Linguistic Theory. Oxford: Clarendon Press, 1989.

Thompson, G. Introducing Functional Grammar. London: Edward and Arnold, 1996.

Thornborrow, J. et al. Stylistics for Students of Language and Literature. London: Routledge, 1998.

Trask, R. L. Historical Linguistics. London: Edward Arnold, 1996.

Ungerer, F & H. J. Schmid. An Introduction to Cognitive Linguistics. London: Longman, 1996.

Verschuren, J. Understanding Pragmatics. London: Arnold, 1999.

Waugh, L. R. "Degrees of Iconicity in the Lexicon". Journal of Pragmatics 22 (1994), 55-70.

Wray, A. et al. Projects in Linguistics: A Practical Guide to Researching Language. London: Edward Arnold, 1998.

Wright, L. et al. Stylistics: A Practical Coursebook. London: Routledge, 1996.

Wu, Guo. Information Structure in Chinese. Beijing: Peking University Press, 1998.

Yan, Shiqing. Metaphor, Metaphorization and Demetaphorization. Suzhou: Suzhou University Press, 2000.

Yang, Lili. Ideational Metaphor in English: A Fundamental Study. Ph.D Dissertation. Guangzhou: Zhongshan University, 1997.

Yu, Ning. The Contemporary Theory of Metaphor: A Perspective from Chinese. Amsterdam: John Benjamins Publishing

Company, 1998.

Zaitseva, V. "The Metaphoric Nature of Coding: Toward a Theory of Utterance". Journal of Pragmatics 22 (1994), 103-126.

Zhang, Keding. A Contrastive Study of the Focusing Devices in English and Chinese. Ph.D Dissertation. Guangzhou: Zhongshan University, 1995.

Zhang, Yunfei. An Introduction to Modern English Lexicology. Beijing: Beijing Normal University Press, 1987.

毕继万. 跨文化非语言交际. 北京：外语教学与研究出版社，1999.

薄　冰. 高级英语语法. 北京：高等教育出版社，1990.

曹务堂. 隐喻的认知性立体透视.《外语与外语教学》1999（3），49-53.

陈道明，从习语的可分析性看认知语言学的隐喻能力观.《外国语》1998（6），20-26.

谌华玉，OVER 概念意义的隐喻化延伸扩展.《外国语》1998（6），27-31.

陈嘉映. 说隐喻，《外国哲学》2003（2），10-24.

陈建民. 中国语言与中国社会. 广州：广东教育出版社，1999.

陈汝东. 认知修辞学. 广州：广东教育出版社，2001.

陈松岑. 语言变异研究. 广州：广东教育出版社，1999.

陈廷祐. 英文汉译技巧. 北京：外语教学与研究出版社，2001.

程　工. 语言共性论. 上海：上海外语教育出版社，1999.

程琪龙. 认知语言学概论. 北京：外语教学与研究出版社，2001.

程琪龙. 语言认知与隐喻.《外国语》2002（1），46-52.

程雨民. 语言系统及其运作. 上海：上海外语教育出版社，1997.

楚明锟. 逻辑学. 开封：河南大学出版社，2000.

丁尔苏. 语言的符号性. 北京：外语教学与研究出版社，2000.

董宏乐. 论科技语言的隐喻性.《外语学刊》1999（3），11-16.

范文芳. 名词化隐喻的语篇衔接功能.《外语研究》1999（1），9-12.

范文芳. 英语语气隐喻. 《外国语》2000（4），29-33.
范　晓. 三个平面的语法观. 北京：北京语言学院出版社，1996.
范　晓. 汉语的句子类型. 太原：书海出版社，1998.
方经民. 汉语语法变换研究. 郑州：河南人民出版社，2000.
方克平、章振群. 类比：结构分析与明喻、暗喻之辩异.《外语与外语教学》1999（7），11-14.
冯友兰. 中国哲学简史. 北京：北京大学出版社，2000.
冯志纯、周行健. 新编现代汉语多功能词典. 北京：当代中国出版社，1995.
高葆泰. 语法修辞六讲. 银川：宁夏人民出版社，1981.
高一虹. 语言文化差异的认知与超越. 北京：外语教学与研究出版社，2000.
耿占春. 隐喻. 北京：东方出版社，1993.
桂诗春. 心理语言学. 上海：上海外语教育出版社，1985.
桂诗春. 应用语言学. 长沙：湖南教育出版社，1988.
桂诗春. 实验心理语言学纲要. 长沙：湖南教育出版社，1991.
桂诗春、宁春岩. 语言学方法论. 北京：外语教学与研究出版社，1997.
郭聿楷、何英玉. 语义学概论. 北京：外语教学与研究出版社，2002.
何桂金. 英语句法新编. 重庆：重庆大学出版社，1998.
何兆熊. 语用学概要. 上海：上海外语教育出版社，1997.
何自然. 语用学概论. 长沙：湖南教育出版社，1988.
何自然. 语用学与英语学习. 上海：上海外语教育出版社，1997.
何自然、冉永平. 语用与认知——关联理论研究. 北京：外语教学与研究出版社，2001.
胡文仲. 跨文化交际学概论. 北京：外语教学与研究出版社，1999.
胡裕树、范晓. 动词研究. 开封：河南大学出版社，1995.
胡壮麟. 语篇的衔接与连贯. 上海：上海外语教育出版社，1994.

胡壮麟. 语法隐喻,《外语教学与研究》1996（4），1-7.
胡壮麟，语言·认知·隐喻，《现代外语》1997（4），50-57.
胡壮麟. 有关语用学隐喻观的若干问题.《外语与外语教学》1998（1），7-10.
胡壮麟. 评语法隐喻的韩礼德模式.《外语教学与研究》2000a（2），88-94.
胡壮麟. 隐喻与文体.《外语研究》2000b（2），10-17.
胡壮麟. 功能主义纵横谈. 北京：外语教学与研究出版社，2000c.
胡壮麟. 诗性隐喻.《山东外语教学》2003（1），3-8.
胡壮麟、朱永生、张德禄. 系统功能语法概论. 长沙：湖南教育出版社，1989.
黄国文. 语篇分析概要. 长沙：湖南教育出版社，1988.
黄汉生. 现代汉语·语法修辞. 北京：书目文献出版社，1981.
贾彦德. 汉语语义学. 北京：北京大学出版社，1999.
姜丽蓉、李学谦. 简析英语比喻表达形式.《外国语》1995（5），32-36.
蒋　勇. 文学和日常话语中虚拟空间的认知能量.《外语教学与研究》2000（4），261-266.
金定元. 对隐喻运作机制的语言学探讨.《贵州大学学报》（社科版）1997（4），89-92.
蓝　纯. 从认知角度看汉语的空间隐喻.《外语教学与研究》1999（4），7-15.
郎天万、蒋勇. 从认知角度拓展韩礼德等对英语语法概念隐喻的分析.《四川外语学院学报》1997（4），30-36.
雷　馨. 英语分类句型. 北京：商务印书馆，1979.
黎昌抱. 英语修辞格新探. 长春：吉林出版社，2001.
李福印. 研究隐喻的主要学科.《四川外语学院学报》2000（4），44-49.
李国南. 英、汉习用性比喻中的喻体比较与翻译.《外国语》1992

（5），37-42.

李国南. 英汉修辞格对比研究. 福州：福建人民出版社，1999.

李明洁. 图式理论与隐喻中“相似即同一”之说.《修辞学习》1997（6），8-9.

李鑫华、李琼. 英语隐喻论.《湖北师范学院学报》（哲社版）1996（5），67-72.

李秀丽. 隐喻研究的误区.《四川外语学院学报》2002（1），87-89.

李秀林、王于、李淮春.《辩证唯物主义和历史唯物主义原理》，北京：中国人民大学出版社，1991.

李英哲. 汉语历时共时语法论集. 北京：北京语言文化大学出版社，2001.

李勇忠、李春华. 认知语境与概念隐喻.《外语与外语教学》2001（6），26-28.

李幼蒸. 理论符号学导论. 北京：社会科学文献出版社，1999.

连淑能. 英语含非人称主语句子的汉译.《翻译通讯》1983（6），22-25.

梁振中. 英语句型. 南宁：广西人民出版社，1984.

林书武.《隐喻：其认知力与语言结构》评介.《外语教学与研究》1994（4），62-63.

林书武.《隐喻与象似性》评介.《国外语言学》1995a（3），40-42.

林书武.《隐喻与认知》评介.《外语教学与研究》1995b（4），70-72.

林书武.《隐喻的一个具体运用——语言的隐喻基础》评介.《外语教学与研究》1996（2），66-70.

林书武. 国外隐喻研究综述.《外语教学与研究》1997a（1），11-19.

林书武. 小 Gibbs 的《思维的比喻性》评介.《外语教学与研究》1997b（2），66-68.

林书武. “愤怒”的概念隐喻：英语、汉语语料.《外语与外语教学》1998（2），9-13.

林书武. 隐喻研究的基本现状、焦点及趋势。《外国语》2002（1），38-45.

林肖瑜. 隐喻的抽象思维功能. 《现代外语》1994（4），41-46, 61.

林玉霞. 英语中 A and B is X 表达方式的隐喻特征. 《外语与外语教学》2000（3），17-19，23.

刘大为. 比喻、近喻与自喻：辞格的认知论研究. 上海：上海外语教育出版社，2001.

刘光耀、姜玲. 从语境看行为主语译为状语从句的技巧. 《中国科技翻译》2000（4），21-22.

刘光耀、史厚敏. 英语名词·名词词组·名词分句. 开封：河南大学出版社，1996.

刘　坚. 二十世纪的中国语言学. 北京：北京大学出版社，1998.

刘宓庆. 当代翻译理论. 北京：中国对外翻译出版公司，1999.

刘润清. 西方语言学流派. 北京：外语教学与研究出版社，1995.

刘永耕. 隐喻的逻辑语义基础. 《修辞学习》1997（4），12-13.

刘涌泉、乔毅. 应用语言学. 上海：上海外语教育出版社，1991.

刘宇红. Congruence 浅议. 《外国语》2001（6），43-48.

刘振前. 隐喻的传统理论与理解模式. 《外语与外语教学》2000（10），18-21.

刘振前、时小英. 隐喻的文化认知本质与外语教学. 《外语与外语教学》2002（2），17-34.

刘正光. 名词动用过程中的隐喻思维. 《外语教学与研究》2000（5），335-339.

陆国强. 现代英语词汇学. 上海：上海外语教育出版社，1983.

陆国强. 英汉和汉英语义结构对比. 上海：复旦大学出版社，1999.

吕叔湘. 中国文法要略. 北京：商务印书馆，1982.

吕叔湘. 汉语语法论文集. 北京：商务印书馆，1984.

吕叔湘（译），赵元任（著）. 汉语口语语法. 北京：商务印书馆，1979.

马清华. 隐喻意义的取象与文化认知. 《外语教学与研究》2000（4），267-272.

马清华. 文化语义学. 南昌：江西人民出版社，2000.

马松亭. 汉语语法修辞. 济南：山东人民出版社，1981.

毛永波. 隐喻扩展与义项建立. 《中国辞书学文集》中国辞书学会学术委员会. 北京：外语教学与研究出版社，2000.

缪锦安. 汉语语义结构和补语形式. 上海：上海外语教育出版社，1990.

宁全新. “Anger”与隐喻. 《外国语》1998（5），69-72.

牛保义. 英汉语句型对比. 开封：河南大学出版社，1997.

潘文国. 汉英语对比纲要. 北京：北京语言文化大学出版社，1997.

庞人琪. 英语转换修辞句法. 北京：北京师范大学出版社，1989.

彭聃龄. 普通心理学（修订版）. 北京：北京师范大学出版社，2001.

彭文钊. 隐喻：认知与阐释.《解放军外语学院学报》1999（1），39-43.

彭宣维. 英汉语篇综合对比. 上海：上海外语教育出版社，2000.

彭玉海. 动词语义结构的隐喻机制. 《四川外语学院学报》2003（2），89-92.

彭增安. 隐喻的作用机制. 《修辞学习》1998（5），29-30.

戚雨村. 现代语言学的特点与发展趋势. 上海：上海外语教育出版社，1997.

任学良. 汉英比较语法. 北京：中国社会科学出版社，1981.

单俊毅. 英语隐喻释义三步法.《国外外语教学》1995（3），13-14，48.

申小龙. 语言与文化的现代思考. 郑州：河南人民出版社，2000.

申雨平. 西方翻译理论精选. 北京：外语教学与研究出版社，2002.

沈家煊. 转指与转喻. 《当代语言学》1999（1），1-9.

沈家煊(译). 戴维・克里斯特尔(编). 《现代语言学词典》，北京：商务印书馆，2000.

史有为. 从语义信息到类型比较. 北京：北京语言文化大学出版社，2001.

石毓智. 《女人，火，危险事物——范畴揭示了思维的什么奥秘》评介. 《国外语言学》1995（2），17-22.

石毓智. 肯定与否定的对称与不对称. 北京：北京语言文化大学出版社，2001.

束定芳. 亚里斯多德与隐喻研究. 《外语研究》1996a（1），13-17.

束定芳. 论现代隐喻学的目标、方法和任务. 《外国语》1996b（2），9-16.

束定芳. 隐喻的语用学研究. 《外语学刊》1996c（2），35-39，44.

束定芳. 理查兹的隐喻理论. 《外语研究》1997（3），24-27，32.

束定芳. 论隐喻的本质与语义特征. 《外国语》1998（6），10-19.

束定芳. 论隐喻的理解过程及其特点. 《外语教学与研究》2000a（4），253-260.

束定芳. 隐喻学研究. 上海：上海外语教育出版社，2000b.

束定芳. 现代语义学. 上海：上海外语教育出版社，2000c.

束定芳. 论隐喻的认知功能. 《外语研究》2001a（2），28-31.

束定芳. 中国语用学研究论文精选. 上海：上海外语教育出版社，2001b.

束定芳. 论隐喻与明喻的结构及认知特点. 《外语教学与研究》2003（2），102-107.

苏晓军、张爱玲. 概念整合理论的认知. 《外国语》2001（3），31-33.

孙梅琳. 英语科技文章中的认知性隐喻及其翻译.《上海科技翻译》1996（4），8-10.

陶文好. 论 OVER 的空间和隐喻认知. 《外语与外语教学》1997（4），31-33.

陶文好. 几个方位介词对 TR 和 LM 空间意义的影响. 《外语与外语教学》1998（9），18-20.

陶文好. 论 UP 的空间和隐喻意义认知. 《外语学刊》2000（4），

13-17.
倜 西、董乐山等.《英汉翻译手册》，北京：商务印书馆国际有限公司，2002.
汪榕培. 英语词汇学研究. 上海：上海外语教育出版社，2000.
汪榕培、李冬. 实用英语词汇学. 沈阳：辽宁人民出版社，1983.
汪榕培、卢晓娟. 英语词汇学教程. 上海：上海外语教育出版社，1997.
汪少华. 隐喻推理机制的认知性透视.《外语与外语教学》2000（10），14-17.
汪少华. 合成空间理论对隐喻的阐释力.《外国语》2001（3），37-43.
王葆华、梁晓波. 隐喻研究的多维视野——介绍隐喻学研究.《外语教学与研究》2001（3），397-398.
王 斌. 交织与隐喻的比较研究.《外语学刊》2001（1），48-53.
王 斌. 隐喻系统的整合翻译.《中国翻译》2002（2），24-28.
王初明. 应用心理语言学. 长沙：湖南教育出版社，1990.
王逢鑫. 英语同义表达法. 北京：外文出版社，1999.
王福祯. 英语句子辞典. 成都：四川辞书出版社，2002.
王 钢. 普通语言学基础. 长沙：湖南教育出版社，1988.
王菊泉. 关于英汉语法比较的几个问题，《外语教学与研究》1982（4），1-9.
王 力. 中国现代语法. 北京：商务印书馆，1985.
王铭玉. 隐喻与换喻. /99 中国博士论坛. 张后尘、胡壮麟. 北京：外语教学与研究出版社，2001，165-176.
王 诺. 原始思维与神话的隐喻.《外国文学评论》1998（3），125-131.
王松亭. 隐喻的哲学分析.《解放军外国语学院学报》1995（6），12-15.
王松亭. 隐喻的感悟及其文化背景.《外语学刊》1996（4），63-66.

王松亭. 隐喻与言语行为. 《外语学刊》1998（4），43-47.

王松亭. 俄汉语中隐喻共性现象对比研究.《解放军外国语学院学报》1999（5），15-17.

王松亭. 浅谈语境因素对隐喻的影响和制约作用. 《外语研究》2000（4），19-24.

王文斌. 论隐喻中的始源之源. 《外语论坛》2003（1），22-27.

王希杰. 修辞学通论. 南京：南京大学出版社，1996.

王希杰. 修辞学导论. 杭州：浙江教育出版社，2000.

王　寅、李弘. 中西隐喻对比及隐喻工作机制分析. 《解放军外国语学院学报》2003（2），6-10.

王宗炎. 语言问题探索. 上海：上海外语教育出版社，1985.

王宗炎. 语言学与语言的应用. 上海：上海外语教育出版社，1998.

王佐良. 英语文体学论文集. 北京：外语教学与研究出版社，1980.

王佐良、丁往道. 英语文体学引论. 北京：外语教学与研究出版社，1987.

温科学. 英汉隐喻对比研究：隐喻的共根. 《外语教学》1995（3），30-36.

吴　莉. 英语管道隐喻的结构探微. 《外语学刊》1999（3），5-10.

伍谦光. 语义学导论. 长沙：湖南教育出版社，1988.

伍铁平. 模糊语言学. 上海：上海外语教育出版社，1999.

席建国、马苏勇. 英语无灵句与汉语有灵句的句法对比及翻译. 《西安外国语学院学报》2002（1），26-28.

谢之君. 隐喻：从修辞格到认知. 《外语与外语教学》2000（3），9-12.

熊学亮. 认知语用学概论. 上海：上海外语教育出版社，1999.

许国璋. 许国璋论语言. 北京：外语教学与研究出版社，1991.

徐莉娜. 隐喻的审美取向与跨文化交际. 《修辞学习》1998（3），6-7.

徐烈炯. 生成语法理论. 上海：上海外语教育出版社，1990.

徐烈炯. 共性与个性——汉语语言中的争议. 北京：北京语言文化大学出版社，1999.
徐盛桓. 语用问题研究. 开封：河南大学出版社，1996a.
徐盛桓. 会话含义理论的新发展. 开封：河南大学出版社，1996b.
徐友渔等. 语言与哲学. 北京：三联书店，1996.
徐有志. 现代英语文体学. 开封：河南大学出版社，1992.
许余龙. 对比语言学概论. 上海：上海外语教育出版社，1992.
许余龙. 隐喻的特征与分类. 《外语研究》2000（4），15-18.
严世清. 隐喻理据史探. 《外国语》1995（5），27-31.
严世清、董宏乐、吴蔚. 系统功能语言学理论的发展和应用. 《外语教学与研究》2000（2），82-87.
杨成虎. 隐喻解释的语义协调论. 《外语学刊》2000（4），19-22.
杨成虎. 隐喻研究背景下修辞格的重新归类问题.《四川外语学院学报》2002（1），90-92.
杨莉藜. 英汉互译教程（上、下）. 开封：河南大学出版社，1993.
杨信彰. 隐喻的两种解释. 《外语与外语教学》1998（10），4-7.
叶蜚声、徐通锵. 语言学纲要. 北京：北京大学出版社，1997.
俞建章、叶舒宪. 符号：语言与艺术. 上海：上海人民出版社，1988.
于 晓等（译），恩斯特·卡西尔（著）. 语言与神话. 北京：三联书店，1988.
袁 辉. 比喻. 合肥：安徽人民出版社，1982.
袁 辉. 二十世纪的汉语修辞学. 太原：书海出版社，2000.
袁毓林. 语言的认知研究与计算分析. 北京：北京大学出版社，1998.
张 蓓. 试论隐喻的认知力和文化阐释功能. 《外语教学》1998（2），14-16，32.
张道真. 现代英语用法词典（重排本）. 北京：外语教学与研究出版社，1994.
张道真. 实用英语语法. 北京：外语教学与研究出版社，1995.

张后尘、胡壮麟. 99 中国博士论坛. 北京：外语教学与研究出版社，2001.
张　今. 文学翻译原理. 开封：河南大学出版社，1987.
张　今. 英语句型的动态研究. 开封：河南大学出版社，1990.
张　今. 思想模块假说. 开封：河南大学出版社，1997.
张　今、陈云清. 英汉比较语法纲要. 北京：商务印书馆，1981.
张　今、刘光耀. 英语抽象名词研究. 开封：河南大学出版社，1996.
张　今、张克定. 英汉语信息结构对比研究. 开封：河南大学出版社，1998.
张培成. 关于 Metaphorical Concept 的几点思考.《外语与外语教学》1998（10），11-13.
章振邦. 新编英语语法教程. 上海：上海外语教育出版社，1983.
章振邦. 新编英语语法（上、下册）. 上海：上海译文出版社，1995.
赵敦华. 现代西方哲学新编. 北京：北京大学出版社，2000.
赵世开. 美国语言学简史. 上海：上海外语教育出版社，1989.
赵世开. 汉英对比语法文集. 上海：上海外语教育出版社，1999.
赵艳芳. 语言的隐喻认知结构. 《外语教学与研究》1995（3），7-72.
赵艳芳. 认知的发展与隐喻. 《外语与外语教学》1998（10），8-10.
赵英玲. 英语空间隐喻的特性分析. 《外语学刊》1999（3），17-21.
中国辞书学会学术委员会. 中国辞书学文集. 北京：外语教学与研究出版社，2000.
周　榕. 隐喻认知基础的心理现实性——时间的空间隐喻表征的实验证据. 《外语教学与研究》2001（2），88-93.
邹世诚. 实用英语句型变换. 南宁：广西人民出版社，1980.
朱德熙. 现代汉语语法研究. 北京：商务印书馆，1980.
朱德熙. 语法讲义. 北京：商务印书馆，1982.
朱小安. 试论隐喻概念. 《解放军外国语学院学报》1994（3），

12-17.
朱小安. 论隐喻的跨社会文化背景问题. 《解放军外国语学院学报》1995（2），18-24.
朱小安. 隐喻的替代理论评析. 《解放军外国语学院学报》1998（1），8-12.
朱小安. 隐喻的转换生成语法解释. 《解放军外国语学院学报》1999（5），10-14.
朱晓亚. 现代汉语句模研究. 北京：北京大学出版社，2001.
朱永生. 英语中的语法比喻现象. 《外国语》1994（1），8-13.
朱永生、严世清. 语法隐喻理论的理据和贡献.《外语教学与研究》2000（2），95-102.
朱永生、严世清. 系统功能语言学多维思考. 北京：外语教学与研究出版社，2001.
朱 跃. 论英语修辞格“言外之意”赖以生存的条件.《外语教学》1996（3），12-15.
祝畹瑾. 社会语言学概论. 长沙：湖南教育出版社，1992.
左思民. 汉语语用学. 郑州：河南人民出版社，2000.

后　记

《英汉隐喻句对比研究》是以我的同名博士论文为基础修改而成的。

回忆论文的写作过程，首先应该感谢我的导师张今先生。他当时虽然已是70多岁高龄，仍然认真、仔细、耐心、及时地指导我的写作，不仅帮助我顺利地完成了论文写作，而且给了我很大的鼓励。此次，先生又亲自为本书作序，使我深感学术界前辈对后辈的殷殷期待之意，拳拳爱护之心。

我也深深地感谢河南大学外语学院的吴雪莉先生、徐盛桓先生、徐有志先生、王宝童先生、刘光耀先生和张克定先生。吴雪莉、刘光耀二位先生是我的硕士论文导师，这些年来他们一直关注着我的生活、工作、学习和科研，我也经常得到他们的教诲，使我的学术探索少走了许多弯路。我在《外语教学》1989年第3期发表的第一篇文章"英语复合疑问句"就是在刘光耀先生指导下撰写的。之后，我们又合作发表过两篇文章："从语境看行为主语译为状语从句的技巧"（《中国科技翻译》2000年第4期）；"系统对应说与转化机制"（《河南大学学报》2000年第3期）。我2002年出版的《英语系统对应说研究》一书也承蒙刘光耀先生全文审校。

读博期间，徐盛桓先生的统计语言学、语用学、功能语言学，徐有志先生的现代英语文体学，刘光耀先生的篇章语言学，张克定先生的当代语言学等课程都使我受益匪浅。论文初稿完成后，承蒙王宝童先生、刘光耀先生、张克定先生全文阅读，并提出宝贵的修改意见和建议。吴雪莉先生更是在百忙之中抽出时间通读论文终稿形成定稿。

对我的论文，新加坡国立大学石毓智先生和解放军外国语学院潘永樑先生均提出过富有启发性的建议。论文完成后，广东外语外贸大学何自然教授、解放军外国语学院潘永樑教授和严辰松教授、厦门大学连淑能教授、苏州大学严世清教授和辛斌教授以及河南大学张克定教授和刘光耀教授评阅了我的论文。他们给论文以较高的评价，同时也提出了宝贵的意见和建议，不仅使我顺利地通过了论文答辩并获得博士学位，对此次论文修改成书也提供了极大的帮助。我衷心地感谢他们。

论文写作过程中，薛玉凤博士帮助我在北京图书馆、北京语言文化大学图书馆复印了很多相关资料，使我节省了许多时间。苏州科技大学陈广平先生当时在荷兰访学，也帮我收集了不少相关资料。我衷心地感谢他们。

此次论文修改成书，得到了河南大学外语学院和河南大学出版社领导的积极支持和具体帮助，外语学院提供了资助。责任编辑薛巧玲女士更是付出了艰辛的劳动。我真诚地感谢他们。

姜　玲
2008 年 2 月 28 日
于河南大学